6

STARTLING
BEAUTY

STARTLING BEAUTY

My Journey from Rape to Restoration

HEATHER GEMMEN

LIFE JOURNEY®

Bringing Home the Message for Life

An Imprint of Cook Communications Ministries
COLORADO SPRINGS, COLORADO • PARIS, ONTARIO
KINGSWAY COMMUNICATIONS, LTD., EASTBOURNE, ENGLAND

Life Journey® is an imprint of Cook Communications Ministries
Colorado Springs, Colorado 80918
Cook Communications, Paris, Ontario
Kingsway Communications, Eastbourne, England

First printing, 2004
Printed in the United States of America
4 5 6 7 8 9 10 Printing/Year 08 07 06 05 04

Editor: Mary McNeil
Cover Design: Marks & Whetstone
Cover Photo: © Cook Ministries by Gaylon Wampler
Interior Design: Lori Jackson

Library of Congress Cataloging-in-Publication Data

Gemmen, Heather.
  Startling beauty : my journey from rape to restoration / Heather Gemmen.
    p. cm.
  ISBN 0-7814-4028-9 (hardcover)
  1. Gemmen, Heather. 2. Christian biography--United States. 3.
Rape--Religious BR1725.G42A3 2004
277.3'082'092--dc22

                              2003020278

Steve,
Dedicating this book to you
is merely a reflection of my promise
to dedicate my love and life to you.

Many thanks to...

Mary McNeil, my excellent editor and best friend:
for reminding me that since God has called me to this task,
he will equip me to do it.

Dan Benson:
for your gentle but persistent nudges toward excellence.

Jeannie St. John Taylor, my writing coach:
for sharing your time and expertise to help shape this book.

Barb Reinhard and Vicki Caruana, my critique group:
for helping me craft words and ideas.

Bob Bever:
for catching the vision of the ministry of this book
and for passing it on to others.

Kim Brandon and Jeff Barnes:
for your expertise and your encouragement.

The entire team at Cook, especially
Terry Whalin, Janet Lee, Craig Bubeck, Jeff Dunn,
Michelle Lowder, Phyllis Williams, Karen Athen, Joni Costa,
Michele Tennesen, Kerry Park, Susan Parsons, Lori Jackson,
Dick Frieg, Ted Ehrlichman, Ken Lorenz, Les Jones,
Mary Chapman, Jeff Ray,
Chris Robinette, David Cura, Kelly Becker,
Patsy Edwards, Jeff Francisco, Jeremy Potter,
Pam Steinberg, Sue Giordano, Pete Zickefoose, Keith Franklin,
Mike Mason, Kathy Guist, Judy Krafchak.

Ray and Linda Bert, Dan Lenahan, and Danny and Mickey Jantz,
my prayer group:
for praying this book into existence.

CONTENTS

POETRY

How else will you rape

my life?

P oetry is escape into truth." She smiles sadly as she
   reads, and the wrinkles on her face deepen. She does
not look at the other members of our small writers' group
gathered in her immaculate home. We know we are the
privileged few to enter her truth.

The group sits silently, savoring language, slowly building
the stack of word pictures into an invisible pile before us.

"Poetry articulates abstraction." He is young and white and
confident. Once he had terrified us with a short story about
what he would do if he were God.

"A poem laughs at despair." Tasha smiles discreetly at me,
and I have to take a deep breath. She knows which poem I will
be reading tonight.

"The poet coaxes a soft brook out of the frothing river of
words." She teaches kindergarten and serves as an elder at her
church. Her laughter is as beautiful as her sentences.

"The poet is a sagacious fool." Blonde dreadlocks bounce as
this newlywed grins around the circle. Her favorite word is *paradox*.

I watch the faces around me and then offer my interpretation: "A poem is the place where familiar beauty becomes startling."

Some of us barely sit in our hardback chairs, as if ready to spring into the places we have created. Some of us retreat into the cushions of the oversized couch, as if longing to fade away from reality. Some of us peer into the eyes of the others, as if expecting to find ourselves there. All of us reach into the stack of words piled in front of us and sift through it, passionately searching our souls.

These are my sisters and brothers. They will understand. When the silence empties, I clear my throat. It is my turn to read first. Tonight I will read out my soul.

For three years our carefully crafted words had brought our unnamed group to intimacy deeper than lovers, and yet I had never revealed to them my secret. Tasha knew the story—had helped carry me through it—but the others here had unwittingly provided a haven for me from the many who knew.

I speak over the thick sound of my fear.

Sire:
Strange that I should remember you …
You whose face I never saw,
Whose words I barely understood.
Your life crossed mine for mere moments.

I'm sure by now you have forgotten …
You whose breath reeked of beer,
Whose words slurred almost beyond comprehension.
You had no idea what you were doing.

I know what you have done …
You stole my courage;

Your words, filthy and threatening, penetrated my soul.
I grasp in vain at a missing part of myself.

How could you not have known?
You scorned a closed door;
You scarred me with your words.
I can still feel the knife pressed against my throat.

I won't forget your laughter ...
You who slapped me when I begged to pray,
Whose words mocked what could have set you free.
I did still pray.

And there is more that you don't know ...
You created more than fear;
Your words are not the only thing you left behind.
I have gained more than I have lost.

Strange that I should forgive you ...
You who do not even know you need it,
Whose words displayed your pathetic need for grace.
You didn't know what you were doing.

The silence throbs once again, and I know my words are between the fingers of my friends, like play dough under the scrutiny of a group of preschoolers. I look at the floor as I wait. How many times had I been taught grace? "God so loved the world that he gave his one and only Son." Familiar. Startling. "I am with you always." Familiar. Startling. "Love your enemies."

I see toes with sky-blue nails wiggle in thick-soled sandals. I nod almost imperceptibly. The postmodern concept that two opposing truths can exist simultaneously is as ancient as God.

But then the soft sound of a full-length skirt rustling in the chair across the room jars me into sudden insecurity. My lofty thoughts are instantly replaced by a frantic concern that I have foolishly opened the door for yet more people to judge me by that which is beyond me.

The cowboy clears his throat. Even he must silently mock my grandiose proclamation of impossible forgiveness.

My fingers fondle the waxy oak at the base of the armrest, and I notice the subtle scent of roses rising from the candle beside me. I am surrounded by flawlessness. I have revealed too much.

Do you see? Your few minutes of ecstasy haunt my entirety. Because of you, even words turn against me.

How else will you rape my life?

My mounting fear creates a foothold for bitterness. Does my forgiveness still hold?

"Read it again, Heather."

I do. This time, I need to pause between words as I fight to get them out of my throat.

When I look up I see emotion, raw and potent, in the faces of these people who love me. I accept the salve of friendship's passionate sorrow and anger, and my soul is caressed smooth again. Bitterness slinks away.

I will not be your captive.

As I listen to my friends' words of encouragement and endearment, anger and sorrow, I am overwhelmed by abundance, I who was once empty and lost. My heart is changed within me.

CHAPTER ONE

STATIC
IN THE
STORM

I reached for
Steve's hand, but he must
not have noticed;
he didn't reach back.

*The havoc you wreaked in my life was not the first storm
I endured. Another struck two years prior to my even being
aware of your existence. It started in the sterility of a doctor's
office. I remember listening to my own heartbeat in the silence
of that examining room.*

W hat's wrong, Maryann?" My whispered words
screamed.

I searched my doctor's face, desperate for the reassurance of
the familiar crinkles around her soft blue eyes. She murmured
some word of comfort, in vain.

A streak of lightning sliced the sky.

"You can't find the heartbeat, can you?" I asked quietly. She
was my friend more often than she was my doctor, and I would
not accept anything less than the full truth.

Maryann looked up at me, and then a smile caught the edge
of her lips. "This baby is definitely your child, Heather. I'm sure
he's dodging the Doppler just to frustrate me."

Her teasing didn't entirely relax me, but I accepted her attempt and tried to smile. "When have I ever frustrated you? I have been the calming source in your life, the sunshine after the rain, the wind beneath your wings—"

"Right." She snorted. "Okay. Maybe *frustrate* is the wrong word for it. Perhaps *torment* would work better."

"Word choice, eh? I knew you would bring it around to Scrabble sooner or later." This was my soul sister. "The only reason I let you win was so Byron wouldn't have to go home ashamed that his esteemed wife was beat by—"

"*Let* me win? You need a psychiatrist, girl, not an obstetrician." Maryann's sandy brown hair maintained a tousled look, whether in the office or at the beach, and her intimidating brilliance was disguised by playful kindness. "Now hush. I want to hear your son."

"It's a girl, Maryann."

"It's a boy. Shh." She raised a finger to her lips and held the silence. Her eyebrows were furrowed. The thunder growled. "So, why didn't Steve come with you today?"

"Come on, Maryann. You know him."

"Yeah, but he hasn't even heard the heartbeat yet."

"I know. But he doesn't take time off work for things like this."

"Did you ask him to come?"

"Well, no. But I know he wouldn't want to."

"Heather," she touched her fingers to her forehead, "you have to do your part. Listen, Steve may be emotionally inaccessible at times—I'll give you that—but that doesn't let you off the hook. You could have at least asked him to come."

"But then he'd come out of obligation and I'd feel guilty."

"Nah. He wouldn't complain."

"Okay. He probably wouldn't say a word, but he'd be ticked off inside. I'm sure he would be."

"You can't jump to conclusions, Heather. It doesn't help."

"Well, what am I supposed to do? I don't know what he's thinking. Either he has no feelings whatsoever or he just doesn't want to tell them to me. Yesterday he felt the baby move for the first time, and I don't even know if he thought that was exciting or not."

"You felt the baby move?"

"Oh, yeah. I forgot to tell you. Lately I've been feeling her flutter all the time, way more than I did with the boys at five months."

"Hmm. I'm surprised. That's early." She rested cool, gloved fingers gently on my belly for a moment. "But, Heather, I'll bet Steve was just as excited as you were. You can't let his poker face fool you."

"Right. If only this *were* a card game. I'd let him win every hand if only we could have some interaction while we played." I waved my hand. "Anyway, I was pretty excited." I put my hand on my belly, too. "Oh, Maryann, I think it must have been her little elbow poking up against me. And she didn't pull away until I moved again."

"No doubt a little boy wanting his daddy." Her words smiled, but Maryann's face looked serious as she spread more gel on my belly and started moving the monitor over it. She turned the volume up and we listened to the swishy noises inside me. After a few minutes she clicked it off and looked at me, but her eyes looked right through me as her thoughts roved. "This Doppler must not be working."

I felt a sprinkle of fear fall over me again. "You still can't find the heartbeat? What are you going to do?"

"Well, I'm going to get a newer one from the other room. This one's older than you are." She winked.

I laughed. But when she left, I lay back, gently massaged the protrusion that represented my baby, and waited for the fluttering to begin. She had measured up exactly right and had moved just yesterday. Nothing could be wrong.

I watched the nimbus clouds pile on top of each other. Occasionally an escaped raindrop splattered against the window, but the sky was not yet ready to release its fury. I've always believed that we each choose our own path, but as I stared out the window in that quiet examining room, I realized for the first time that we don't get to choose the obstacles we face on the journey.

Oh, God, don't let this be my obstacle. Let me learn about life another way.

Maryann was silent for nearly five minutes as she moved the cool plastic plate back and forth over my belly, pushing gently and then more firmly, listening to the creaks and groans, rumbles and churnings.

"Wait. I heard it," I said after an especially loud whoosh.

"No. That did sound somewhat like a baby's heartbeat, but it's actually the blood flow through your arteries. Listen." We heard some more whooshing sounds. "It's much slower than the baby's heartbeat." She waited a moment longer and then turned off the monitor. I watched her long, smooth fingers fold the tool neatly into the drawer and then float upward to slide through the soft curls over her eyes. She glanced at the clock and then put the lid on the gel and straightened the instruments beside it. Finally, she looked at me, pulling the white jacket tight around her athletic shoulders as she crossed her arms in front of her. "Well, Heather, we're going to have to get you to the hospital for an ultrasound."

The storm broke and propelled its wrath against me. I knew the truth without being told.

I have heard the question from little kids and from old ladies: Why does God let bad things happen to good people?

I've known a mother who left her fourteen-month-old son home alone in his crib for sixteen hours; she laughed when the child was taken away from her. Steve and I had chosen names for our baby before she was the size of a pea; before she was as big as a banana, I had blankets and diapers and pajamas folded neatly in the room that would be her home. Our first two children had been conceived accidentally, at times inconvenient for us; we loved them no less for it. This child had been prayed for and anticipated, our reward for a job well done.

The illusion of control shattered before my eyes.

"Don't give up, Heather. We might be able to pick up the heartbeat at the hospital." I nodded heavily and prepared to leave while Maryann personally made arrangements. Just before I left the office, she grabbed my arm and pulled me into a spontaneous hug. She almost squeezed the tears out of me.

Moments after stepping outside, I felt my hair pressed slick against my scalp, but I did not pop open my umbrella or run through the rain. And I sat quietly before I turned on the car. It's hard to believe that God knows our prayers when we do not even know what to say. My wipers slapped the rain that dumped on my windshield, and I thought about the baby pushing up against me the day before. No wonder she hadn't moved away when I touched her. She couldn't.

I called Steve when I got home. "What are we going to do?" I lamented quietly.

Over the thick static threatening our connection, I heard Steve's answer. "We'll go ... hospital like ... said and find out if every ... alright."

I wanted *connection.*

"Oh, Steve, what's going to happen?" The dim yellow glow encircling the porch light was nearly swallowed up by the sheet of rain streaking into it. "What are we going to do?"

Steve didn't hear my question.

"I'll … home in ten minutes and we'll … the boys to … parents' house. Then we'll meet … with Maryann…." The connection was broken.

I set down the phone and stared at my reflection in the window. The paleness of my round face was hidden in the dark glass, but I could see the effects of the rain on my long, straight hair. Dark eyes looked sadly back at me and full lips twisted downward. I leaned my forehead against the cold window. *Does rain hurt when it smacks against a window? Does it want to mingle with the brown hair that is pressed into the glass?* The rain and I, like my husband and I, nearly touched each other.

When Steve came home, he threw an odd expression toward the red spot on my forehead—and I felt foolish for my meandering thoughts.

An hour later I lay on a doctor's table again, intently watching the screen, asking the technician many questions about what I saw as he wiggled the camera over my belly. He pointed the heart out to me when I asked: a little black blip on the screen, perfectly still. He must have known I understood my baby's status, but I didn't cry. Steve stood silently by my side while I joked about having to pee.

The curse of gregarious people is that our extroversion sometimes shows up at inappropriate times. I remember respecting Steve's taciturn nature, maybe for the first time since our wedding, when our neighbor showed up at our door a few years ago, her bag stuffed with clothes and her left eye badly swollen. "Can I stay with you a few days?" she asked. I, embarrassingly, responded with delighted enthusiasm to the opportunity for enjoyable company rather than, like Steve, extending hospitality and then sitting back quietly, ready to listen to words that would express her apparent suffering.

In this situation, as I stared at the screen that proved my

baby had died, I used humor as a shield. Laughter might keep away sorrow.

The technician told us to wait while he took the pictures to the doctor. We waited, and my own black blip of a heart could stand no more. Resistance crumbled. I had struggled against the sweeping sorrow—and felt as if I were pushing my way through the wind that shook the world outside—but now I wept. Our precious baby had died.

When Maryann entered the little room only minutes later, looking very disturbed, she knew she was saved the work of breaking the news to us. Instead she sat down and waited until I had finished sobbing.

"Maryann," I croaked, "do you know if it was a girl or a boy?"

Maryann shook her head. "I don't think we got a clear view of that from the ultrasound"—I nodded with acceptance—"but we'll find out in a little while."

A blast of truth hit me. The storm wasn't over yet.

I craned my neck back to see him, but Steve looked straight ahead as he pushed me in a wheelchair down the hallway. Oddly, I felt surprised by his perfect features that I had come to know so well: soft brown hair falling neatly into place; thick eyelashes extending over deep brown eyes; muscular arms complementing his slim body; tall legs moving confidently forward.

The storm did not seem to touch him.

Would resistance eventually crumble for him, or did he have nothing to resist?

We passed a few moms groaning in the pains of labor, the nursery housing several newborns, and the nurses' station where one woman grinned at me as we descended to the far end of the obstetrics hall.

I stopped looking around. Instead, I ventured back to the moments (was it only a few hours ago?) that I had pressed my head against the glass, comparing my marriage to raindrops on a window—and no longer felt foolish. Rather, I envisioned myself punching the glass, shattering it, so the rain, so Steve's love, could drench me.

I envisioned but did nothing more.

Maryann came in and sat down with us again. She didn't seem in a hurry to start the procedure, and I was thankful for that. Things were happening much too quickly already.

"I'm going to give you medication to induce labor," Maryann told me. "We will wait for full dilation to occur and for your water to break, and then you will deliver this baby as if everything were normal." She looked at me sympathetically before she continued. "I need to warn you that this will be painful and long. You are physically unprepared for this. Your body thinks it still has a few months to go."

I nodded. For once my body and mind were in agreement.

"I'm sorry, Heather and Steve. This is really tough."

I reached for Steve's hand, but he must not have noticed; he didn't reach back.

Maryann was right. Bare minutes after taking the medication, I felt my first labor pain. I gasped in surprise as I was plunged into an all-night, agonizing ordeal.

When it came time to push, I didn't bother to call for help. Steve sent for a nurse when he saw what was happening. "Try to wait until Maryann gets here, Heather," he begged. But I pushed. *What difference does it make? The baby's dead anyway.*

Maryann came in time to help deliver the placenta and to care for me. The silent infant was set aside.

Exhausted, I closed my eyes and wished for sleep. Maybe now it would all be over. I didn't care about the gender of the baby, about whether or not Steve loved me, about what

Maryann was doing. I had no desire to pray—neither to cry out in anger nor to breathe in God's peace. I just wanted to sleep.

A nurse touched me on the shoulder. I turned, and in her arms was the baby, so tiny, dressed in a blue gown and a white woolen hat far too big for him. "It's a boy. Would you like to hold him?"

A boy? He seemed alien to me, and I could hardly acknowledge that this baby before me was my own child. I shook my head.

But Steve reached out for him. "A boy," he crooned as he pulled back the hat to better see the little head. I watched a half-smile creep over Steve's face, and I couldn't help peeping at our child. He was precious. So delicate and so small. The nurse encouraged us to undress him, to examine him thoroughly, to embrace our little one with the pride only new parents can have. We did, and the nurse left us alone.

I did not feel sad during those brief moments with our son. I had emerged into the calm of the storm. I marveled at how perfectly he was formed, how each of his tiny toes was wrinkled just right, how soft his cheeks felt, how round his belly was. His death did not diminish his beauty.

"You did a great job again, Heather," Steve told me. I soaked up his favor like parched ground soaking in a late summer rain.

"It was worth it." My words surprised me. I looked at the little fingers resting on mine. "An hour ago I wouldn't have said that, but now—well, he is absolutely amazing."

"Yes. Casey is amazing."

We smiled at each other. The rain poured down, and I stood with head back and mouth open to take in as much as I could.

"Steve, would you ever have believed that our hearts could be so full and so empty at the same time?" A beautiful paradox. Steve turned his head to look out the window. I put my hand on his arm. "The emotion is almost too much, isn't it?"

Steve didn't say anything for a moment. Finally, still looking out the window as if preparing to face the storm we were reentering, he shook his head. "I'm confused."

I murmured agreement.

"No, it's different," he said. I couldn't read the look in his eyes when he turned to me. "I don't feel anything at all. I mean, I'm amazed that this child is so perfectly developed, but I don't feel strong love or sadness. I wish I could agree with you that the emotion is too much, but it's not."

I let go of Steve and lifted Casey to my shoulder, patting his back as if listening for a burp. "You must be numb still, from the shock."

"No, it's not that."

We shifted uneasily in the silence.

I made another attempt. "Well, you hadn't even felt the baby move until yesterday. It makes sense that you're not feeling the loss like I am."

He looked out the window again, staring right through the drizzle. "No, it's not that, either." Steve slumped into the stiff hospital chair. "I never feel things strongly. Sometimes I wonder if I'm even able to love at all." He almost whispered the words.

I softly pressed my cheek against Casey's cold body.

Raindrops don't hurt when they smack against a window; they don't even notice the brown hair pressed into the glass. No, I had felt the extent of Steve's rain in his brief smile moments ago.

When the nurse stole into the room a while later, I kissed Casey's cheek and reluctantly handed him over to her. Then I turned my head to sleep. I could not consider my husband's emptiness just yet.

I slept as Steve signed the papers that released our child to the funeral home for cremation and as he made the appropriate phone calls to family and friends. I barely woke when nurses checked my vitals. I slept through visitations from our pastor and friends. I groaned when I had to eat; I cried when I had to urinate; and I bawled when my milk came in.

I laid in bed begging God to transform me into a stoic so I would not have to feel the pain of loss, to help me gain comfort from people's words that little Casey was cuddled safely in his arms, or to convict me that this—like "all things … for those who love him"—would turn out for good.

But grief overcame me. The repercussions of my loss were strewn before me like broken branches on a windswept street.

Steve wheeled me out of the hospital the next day. My arms were full of flowers, cards, and candy, but I held only emptiness.

CHAPTER TWO

HEAVY EMPTINESS

*If God wants us
to stay here, I thought,
we'll just have to
disobey him.*

The extent of the darkness you would deliver a few months from now was beyond my ability to fathom. I thought today I had reached an impenetrable depth already.

I t's negative." I slumped onto the bed.

"I'm surprised." Steve slathered shaving cream on his thick stubble. "You've sure been acting pregnant." His grin was like a stick in the hand of a twelve-year-old boy probing an injured dog. He meant no harm, but I snarled.

"What's that supposed to mean?"

"Oh, don't be so sensitive. I'm kidding."

Our house throbbed with the heavy bass of rap music coming from a car illegally parked at the playground across the street. I watched Steve slice through the foam on his face and wished I could slice through him myself. Instead I rolled over to the window and slammed it shut despite the July afternoon heat — but not before I caught a glimpse of our inner-city neighborhood where litter fluttered in the breeze, houses banged up next to each other, groups of kids loitered beside school fences, and cars squealed and sped their way down the residential streets.

Steve flicked the excess shaving cream off his razor and began washing his face. "After the game, I'm going grocery shopping. Is there anything else you want to add to the list?"

"Steve!" I raised an arm in exasperation. "What is your problem? Didn't you hear what I said? The pregnancy test was negative!" I thought about whipping a pillow at him to wake him up.

"I heard." He dropped beside me on the bed and draped an arm over my belly. "So we keep trying." He kissed my shoulder. "I like trying to get you pregnant." His hand stole under my top.

"Cut it out." I rolled over, turned my back to him, and gave in to my despair. "How can you think about sex at a time like this?"

I could feel him shrug.

"You don't get it, do you?" The windowpane vibrated as it tried to hold out the offensive noise from the street below. "It's been almost a year since Casey died, and I'm still not pregnant. What's wrong with me, Steve?" I whispered.

"Nothing's wrong with you."

"Then why can't I get pregnant?" The words would hardly come out because of the sadness that wallowed in my throat.

I didn't notice Steve's silence until he spoke a few moments later: "Maybe we aren't supposed to have another kid."

"Don't even say that." I turned toward him to search his face. "We'll keep trying."

"I think this is becoming too much for you." Steve looked at his hands. "You don't laugh anymore. I miss that. I want the old you."

It seemed so long ago that I laughed. The Heather who threw spontaneous parties to celebrate someone's promotion or to try out a new recipe or to acknowledge the first snowfall, the

Heather who convinced friends to give up the safety of the bench
for the thrill of the roller coaster and the comfort of the beach
for the fun of the waves, the Heather who turned mundane jobs
into community shindigs—that Heather seemed far removed.

"Maybe we should quit trying," Steve said quietly.

I felt my face contort as I absorbed his words. "Quit? How
can you say that?" Suddenly I hated the intense heat and stood
up to yank the trembling window back open again. "We can't
quit, Steve."

The steady *thud* of a bouncing basketball pounded in my
ears, but Steve's words smacked me in the face: "We have to."

"Steve!" I choked. "Are you kidding?"

"We have two kids already. It feels good to be leaving the
baby stage behind. Besides—" he pointed toward the window
"—we've got to save up enough money to move out of here."

"Yeah, but that doesn't mean—"

"Be realistic."

I stared at my perfectly cool and aloof husband in disbelief.
"But we always said we'd have three." His eyes patronized
me—waiting for me to acknowledge his truth against my
pathetic hope—but I couldn't stop. "You really don't want
another kid?"

"I don't. I'm happy with two."

Happy.

Fleetingly I wondered if it was I, and not Steve, who needed
a pillow whipped at me. But self-pity smothered the joy I longed
to have.

"The emptiness is *heavy,* Steve." I held out my arms. "Can't
you feel it?"

His eyes said no.

I gulped for air. "So all this time you've been hoping the
tests would be negative?" I knew the question was not fair, but
I didn't care.

"Well, it's not —" He pushed himself up on one elbow and tried to touch me. I pulled away.

"I can't believe it." I spat the words at him as the sadness that had been hovering exploded into fragments of anger, pain, betrayal. I couldn't sit near him anymore; I couldn't stand that he peered into me like I was a case study to be figured out. "You really don't care about me, do you?" Hot, angry tears embarrassed me, and I turned my face from him. "Have you ever cared?" From deep in the pillow my smothered voice wailed out to him: "Have you ever cared about anything?" It was the first time I acknowledged the confession he had made at Casey's deathbed — and I used it against him. I hated my own cruelty more than I hated him.

The reflection in the mirror when I looked up showed my red eyes and ugly scowl. I stared at that image of myself and cried bitterly, unguarded. The sorrow spilled out of me like the rap music that spilled out of the Jeep below: harsh and uncensored. Killing. Cursing. Raping. Screaming. The ugliness of words paralleled the ugliness of my despair.

I glanced at Steve beside me on the bed. I knew he wanted to go.

Yes, the emptiness was heavy. It was about time I started helping Steve carry his load. *God, help me.*

A moment later, I heard the bedroom door squeak open. "Mommy?"

I brushed away my tears and held out a hand to four-year-old Chad. "Hi, honey."

"What the matter, Mommy?"

"Oh, Chad, I've been feeling sad. But I'll be better pretty soon, okay?"

"Okay. Mommy, what 'white boy' mean?"

I caught Steve's eye and he shrugged.

"It means that whoever called you that wants to look like you." I justified the loaded statement to myself by claiming rights to protect my child from emotional harm. But Chad didn't question my reasoning.

"Oh. Can I play outside?"

"In the backyard, okay? Don't go into the front yard. And don't wake Simon." He kissed me and ran off. I looked at Steve. "We've got to get out of here, Steve. Yesterday I saw a kid throw sand in Chad's eyes when he was sitting by the sidewalk. They don't want us here."

"Why was he in the front yard?"

"I was working in the flower garden." I shuddered. "Eeh. It was awful. I felt like everyone was looking at me." I sat up and looked out the window. "What do these people do, anyway? They sit on their front porches and watch each other. It gives me the creeps."

"Just forget about the garden," Steve told me.

"Okay. Fine. As soon as we sell the stupid house!"

"Yeah." Steve nodded his head, thinking. "But I don't really want to lower our asking price."

"Who cares about money? What if some gunman comes running through our yard again? We can't live like this."

"Yeah, I know. It's just weird that we've had this house on the market for almost a year and nobody has even looked at it."

I snorted. "It's not weird. I can't believe we were such suckers!"

"I don't know. Maybe God's trying to tell us something."

I cocked an eyebrow. "Like what?"

Steve remained silent for a moment before he spoke: "What if he wants us to stay here?"

He couldn't have meant it. He hated this place more than I did.

We had been living in the house only a couple months when

we were initiated into our neighborhood: We were drinking eggnog and licking the fudge off our fingers at my parents' house hundreds of miles away that Christmas Eve when my dad walked into the room holding out the phone to Steve. "It's the police." The front door of our house had been swinging open, and some officers driving past were suspicious. They entered our home and saw clear evidence of a break-in: shattered glass, an empty entertainment center, a floor strewn with half-emptied drawers. Even our sweaters had been carted off in our laundry baskets.

Steve, sitting in a living room so far away, recognized his own powerlessness to defend his home or to pay retribution to those who violated it. Resentment was born.

One evening a few months later, Steve heard some commotion in the yard. He went to the window and saw some teens slinking over our fence and slipping through our neighbor's back door. "Hey!" he hollered. "What are you guys up to?" The kids scattered. Steve, armed with a baseball bat, followed the intruders, yelling at me to call the police. I did, terrified at what Steve was getting himself into. By the time a unit pulled up, Steve had pinned one of the kids and told him, in his gently intimidating way, that he and his gang were not welcome in our neighborhood.

Now, to think that Steve thought we ought to stay was laughable.

"Yeah, right." I looked out the window at the yellow grass below. "Why would God want us to stay here?"

Steve shrugged and waved the idea away. "I don't know. It's crazy."

I laughed a little too loudly in agreement. *If God wants us to stay here,* I thought, *we'll just have to disobey him.* I had learned enough—too much—during our four long years in the city.

They say the first step to overcoming racism is to admit you have it. Well, then, I was well on my way to recovery.

The black culture that surrounded me seemed nothing short of pathetic, and I had no problem discussing my opinion with anyone who would listen: Two-year-olds wandered unattended at the playground across the street. Teens were getting pregnant or hauled off to jail. The local convenience store was robbed five times in one summer. Murders in our neighborhood didn't even make the evening news. Ebonics was not a course to be studied, but the only language known. Money was spent on stereo systems rather than milk and eggs.

I hadn't expected to feel so bitter against my black neighbors when we moved into the area. I had never had much contact with people outside my Dutch, Christian Reformed circle and assumed all people were just like me, no matter what race they were. So when people more knowing than we were warned us against purchasing the quaint house that was impossibly cheap, we ignored them. Steve loved the economics, and I didn't comprehend the implications of living as a minority.

My naïveté held for a year or so. I loved the river of kids that flooded my home to gush over my pretty house and soft hair and sweet baby. I scoffed at my white friends who advised that I check the pockets of my "darlings" as they walked out the door. I was delighted to see neighbors chatting on porches with as much familiarity as I had had in my small hometown. The richness of community contrasted with the poverty of material wealth. The words and mannerisms of my neighbors intrigued me: I found the black culture to be lovely, beautiful—just as a poet from the countryside would find beauty in the dance of cars moving through a busy intersection. Common beauty was startling through my eyes.

I'm not sure when my attitude changed—maybe I was convinced by the skepticism of others, maybe protective mothering instincts heightened my awareness of danger, maybe I was watching the world instead of heaven—but I lost my innocence by the time Chad turned one: Our family walks eventually started at a distant park rather than our front step; a high wooden fence soon replaced the chain link fence surrounding our backyard; blinds covered the unpainted oak window frames and blocked out the sun.

By the time Chad was two, I had become bitter: I didn't allow neighbor kids to play at our house anymore because too often I couldn't find some of my belongings, and I wanted to rule out theft. Once I took a young boy called Deshawn firmly by his hand and rang his mother's doorbell. The smell of marijuana and the noise of rap fell out of the darkness of her home when she answered the door.

"Hi," I said with tight lips. "I'm your neighbor. I need to tell you that Deshawn may not come on our property anymore. He has broken our porch light twice this week, and he plucks every tulip before it can even open. I am terribly busy with my college classes and raising my own kids, so I don't have time to baby-sit yours." It was my first time on her doorstep, but I didn't stay for chitchat.

As I walked back home, I wondered if I had been too harsh; but it made me angry that she could laze around while I worked so hard. *She doesn't have to be the way she is just because she's black. Look at Tasha!* I muttered to myself. Tasha was my friend who lived on the other side of the schoolyard, provided a well of wisdom from which I often drew, and seemed always to know exactly what I needed to hear. *She pulled herself out of this mess.*

I didn't enjoy my resentment—I hated it—but I didn't know how to change my heart. I wished I could go back to innocence—and I thought I could if only we would move out of this ghetto.

A nyway," I shot at my husband, "now I have another reason for wanting to get out of here." The after-crying breath caught in my chest, and Steve looked at me.

"You know, we can keep trying to have another baby if you think you can handle the stress. It's not like I would hate to have another kid."

It took a few moments for me to answer. "I wasn't crying about that."

"What?" He wearied of these conversations.

"I'm not crying because you don't want a baby," I snuffled. "Okay, it's about that, too, but it's more about us."

Steve closed his eyes. As my emotions snowballed, his tolerance for me dwindled. As he grew colder, I grew more desperate to be understood. "All I'm asking is that you say you love me once in awhile, that you kiss me without wanting sex, that you tell me how you're feeling. Sometimes your eyes hate me, Steve. Am I that awful to live with?"

For the first time, I wanted to know the answer even though I was scared of what I'd hear.

"Oh, honey." Those intolerant eyes softened as they looked at me from beneath long lashes. "I'm sorry." I suppose he meant it, but for once I wasn't ready to hear it. This time I wanted first to understand how to resolve the issue. I had to look away or I would give in, accept the apology, and continue in our well-worn pattern.

"I know. Me too. We're always sorry. But tomorrow everything will be back to how it always is." I watched him sit up slowly and swing his feet over the side of the bed so his broad shoulders faced me. "You'll say that you'll try to be a better husband, but tomorrow I'll still feel like a moron every time you give me that look—you know which one—without saying anything." I touched the thick muscles on his arms and smelled his cologne. My words lost their thrust. "I'll say something, and you'll ignore me or you'll attempt to win the grand prize for insulting me to tears in five words or less." Steve turned around and smiled a little. I wasn't sure if I wanted to kiss him or hit him. "You're such a jerk and I love you so much. I'm sorry I'm such an emotional wreck. But, Steve," —I started to etch my name on his back with my finger— "I really need love from you."

Steve reached for a tissue and handed it to me. "I want things to work between us. Heather," —he paused and I held my breath in anticipation—"I … I will do better, okay?"

"Okay." I tried to smile as I nodded and got out of bed— even though I knew he wouldn't be able to do any better. He wouldn't be able to love me.

"Now, is the grocery list done or do you still want to add stuff?"

I sighed. A plaque hanging over the dresser caught my attention:

> *O Master, grant that I may never seek*
> *so much to be consoled as to console,*
> *to be understood as to understand,*
> *to be loved as to love with all my soul.* *

"It's done," I told him.

"Okay. Say hi to Tasha for me."

I smiled at his retreating back. He was right, and I loved him for knowing me so well: I was aching for some of Tasha's balm.

I picked up the phone as he drove out the driveway.

* Francis of Assisi, "Make Me a Channel of Your Peace"

CHAPTER THREE

PAINFUL HEALING

I grudgingly opened
my eyes and peeked out
from the covers.
The man standing in my
bedroom was not Steve.

*The only white woman among a crowd of black people.
I wonder how long ago you noticed me. I wonder how often you
were watching me. I did not think about that as I sat on the
park bench with Tasha.*

I don't think I can handle this whole marriage thing, Tash!" I wailed as we watched Chad push Simon on the swing. Simon's eyes were bright with delight, and Chad was asking him if he wanted to go higher. Each time Simon swung back, their blond heads would align, and their smiles looked identical.

"Steve's gettin' under your skin, is he?"

"Well, no. I don't know why I'm frustrated with him. He's so wonderful, really."

"Mmm-hmm." Tasha nodded. "He sure do help out a heap around the house. I know many womenfolk who'd give up an arm for a man like that."

"Yeah. And he's so good with the kids."

"What's wrong then? You been fighting?"

"No. It's not that." I sighed heavily. "It's just that it feels like we're not even together." I raised my hands dramatically in the air. "Is it too much to ask him to treat me like a woman instead of a roommate?"

"Romance ain't everything, honey."

"I know. But love is. Besides," I continued, "you know how I always say that our strengths are our weaknesses. Well, that's something Steve doesn't get. He's authentic, but only because he doesn't care what others think of him. He also doesn't care how he makes others feel. I want him to care what people—well, at least what I—think of him."

I might have gone on, but Tasha interrupted me. "Alright. Try single parenting and see if you like that."

"No, I don't want that, of course."

"So, what do ya want?"

I liked Tasha's no-nonsense attitude—though I knew some folks at our church didn't.

Tasha and I had met at Sherman Street Church a couple years earlier. I had been sitting near the back row where I could easily slip out with one of the boys if they needed some extra attention. A second grader had lit the Christ candle during the first verse of the opening hymn. The bulletin that had been placed in our hands after a warm greeting indicated that praise singing came next and that we should stand for this portion of the service. But I didn't need to read the bulletin to cue me in. I shifted Simon to the other arm while I spoke the Lord's Prayer in unison with my brothers and sisters in Christ. I lowered my head respectfully while I received the blessing offered by the pastor. I sat simultaneously with those around me when the homespun quartet walked to the front to offer "special music." This church and its customs were as familiar to me as my own living room.

But then something changed. I glanced over my shoulder when the back door opened silently, and I saw a smashing woman move into the seat in front of my family. Her age was hard to determine because her stylish exterior seemed so much younger than her aura of easy confidence, but I figured she was probably in her early forties. Her ebony skin looked polished against the red velvet dress that clung to her alluring figure. Her full lips were thickly painted to match the long, red fingernails that rested on her folded arms. She briefly surveyed the primarily white congregation that met in the primarily black neighborhood and then began to nod her head in time to the music. As if surprised at their skill, she turned her full attention to the musicians and began to clap so that the whites of her hands slapped loudly in the still room. "Oh yes!" she moaned. "Alleluia!"

If heads turned or if whispers started, I didn't notice. All I saw was hope. The dream of our church, for as long as I had been part of it and despite our long history of failure in achieving the dream, had been to breach the chasm that separated the parish community from the constituents of our church. We wanted this to be the place where all nations could worship together, reconciled with each other and God: the place to set aside our differences as easily as we would take off our winter coats in front of a warm fire. A cozy place. A peaceful place.

We hadn't imagined that racial healing would hurt.

We prayed regularly that people from the neighborhood would join us, and we welcomed them fervently when they trickled in. We couldn't understand why they rarely interacted during the service and even more rarely came back. Personally, I sometimes wondered if the core group of people at Sherman Street—we who developed our mission statement and organized the block parties and attended the evangelism committee meetings—didn't truly represent the church body. It made me uneasy. How could our dream be realized if the majority of the church wanted things to stay the same? It frustrated me. We weren't asking folks to move into the city (heaven knew, if they wanted to do that, they could buy my house); we were asking them, for just one hour of the week, to be welcoming to people different from themselves, to build friendly relationships with the guests.

Ironically, I blamed other people for running off our neighbors, but I never suspected that I was the scariest white of them all. I was the kind of person black people avoided: I knew enough to realize that a problem needed to be solved, but I didn't care enough to find out how to solve it.

In truth, I had been told how to work toward racial healing: build relationships. I had heard it over and over again, at each racial reconciliation meeting I had attended with my other white friends. "The only way to overcome the disease of racism," I had been told, "is to get to know people who are not from your own skin color and culture." But I didn't get it. I thought church, because of the base in faith it provided, was the only place I had to do that. I could see no commonality with my neighbors.

And so, before her seat was warm, this woman whose white teeth flashed and whose large, gold earrings dangled wildly, had unwittingly obliged me to make her acquaintance. I squirmed in my seat, wondering what I would say after the pastor walked to the back door of the sanctuary where he would shake hands with us as we filed slowly out. But I didn't need to worry. As soon as the sermon started, Tasha heard Simon's gurgle and turned around to gush over his soft cheeks and his ready smile. "Can I hold him, honey?" she whispered loudly in her thick black accent. I gladly handed him over and then quietly stole out of my pew and squeezed in beside her. By the time the service was over, Natasha Desiree Peterson had won my heart.

Actually, by the time the service was over, she and I were in the cool basement of the church swapping birthing stories. Steve found us laughing heartily together with Simon snuggled soundly in my new friend's arms and Chad staring adoringly up at her. Honestly, I don't know if our friendship started because I wanted to minister to a guest or because God sent her to reach into my soul and to pull out nuggets I hadn't even known were there. Whatever the reason, a few years later we sat on a park bench deep in conversation.

So what *do* ya want?" she wisely asked me.
"I don't want to be single, that's for sure." I shuddered. "I really don't think I could do it on my own. Especially living here." I saw a black man walking toward us and wished I had a car door to lock. Instead, I got up to help Simon out of the swing.

Tasha folded her arms over the silver hoop piercing her belly button and slowly rocked side to side, humming. Her slim shoulders moved easily under the strings of her halter-top. Chad and Simon ran off to join a group of boys in the sandbox. It seemed apparent that they, at ages four and two, hadn't yet noticed how different they were from their neighbors.

I wandered back to Tasha. "Did you know that we bought our house in the winter? We didn't even realize we were in the 'hood until spring when suddenly the whole tribe swarmed outside and beat their bass drums on their car stereos until winter came again." I laughed.

Tasha didn't. It really was a stupid joke.

"I don't mean *you* when I talk like that, Tash. You're different."
"Am I?"
"Yeah. I don't even think of you as black."
"Just like Steve don't think of you as a woman." Tasha batted her lashes at me and then turned her head to hum some more.

I don't even think of you as black. That wasn't just a bad joke.

That was a revelation of my true self. I hushed and watched the kids for a little while, letting my friend's words sink in. The splinters in my throat from that morning's confrontation with Steve gathered to form a giant lump. My paradigm was shifting.

A boy threw sand at Chad. I almost jumped up, but then I saw Chad grab his own face and pretend to fall over. They both broke out into giggles.

The man I had dodged stood patiently behind a two-year-old girl wearing Winnie-the-Pooh overalls as she painstakingly climbed the ladder to the top of the slide. I watched him hold up his hand protectively as he moved to the foot of the slide and then murmur encouraging words to the delighted child who wouldn't budge.

A sixteen-year-old boy bounced a basketball to a younger boy with the same toothy grin. "You all dat, boy," the older one hollered out. "Yeah, buddy." The younger one dribbled the ball, glanced at his brother, and missed the hoop. The older boy caught the ball and tossed it back. "Try again." The younger boy stuck his tongue between his lips in concentration as he aimed. This time the ball swished through the hoop. They both hooted with pleasure while they ran their hands in a quick succession of motions that ended in a handshake.

As I watched the scenes playing out before me, I found myself thinking that if this were a movie, the camera would be panning from each of the characters in the park to my face, which would be slowly growing more and more pale. The audience would be holding their breath as they squeezed the hand of whomever they were with. "Yes," they would be wanting to shout out at me, "you're getting it!" But instead of feeling the excitement that imaginary viewers might be enjoying over my epiphany, I felt only a sickening twist in my stomach as the implosion that had started that morning continued.

Something needs to change, God. Is it me? Again?

Tasha broke the silence. "So, what started all this trouble with your man?"

I felt dizzy. "It doesn't really matter." I tried to look at her without moving my head. "Oh, Tasha. I'm sorry. I'm just a stupid white person."

She laughed, and it surprised me. It surprised me even more when she scooted closer to me and gave me a sideways hug. "You is stupid, girl, but I still love ya."

I looked at the ebony fingers of her right hand intertwined with the white ones of my left hand. "Look how black you are."

Tasha's voice seemed to vibrate from deep within her chest when she laughed. Usually I have to laugh with her when I hear it. This time I wanted to cry.

Shame overwhelmed me.

"Oh, Tash, I can hardly bear myself. I am so … Oh, Tasha, I'm so racist, aren't I?" Tasha kept her left arm around me while I pulled my hands to my face and curled my shoulders down. "When I was in college I lived with a girl from Nigeria, and I loved feeling so … so cosmopolitan. I thought that meant I wasn't racist." I laughed sourly. "I really didn't get to know her that well."

Tasha was humming again. I noticed the song was an old hymn that we hardly ever sang at Sherman Street: "Let My People Go."

"I thought that since *you're* my friend, I wasn't racist." I laid my head on her shoulder and let myself cry. "I thought that since I was involved in a church that preached racial reconciliation, I wasn't racist." My tears flushed down my face. I grinned through them at Tasha. "Now I'm surprised you keep coming back."

Tasha nodded. "Everybody sure love me at Sherman Street, but I wonder if it ain't just 'cause I'm black. Still, I keep hoping they'll eventually love me for being me."

"I used to love you just because you're black." I blushed at my confession and stared at the dirt under my feet.

Tasha pulled a tissue out of her purse and dabbed my cheeks. "I know, sister. But that's alright. You a changed woman now."

Suddenly, my shame dissipated. I took a deep breath and felt myself straighten and soften at the same time.

"Strange." I suppose I was speaking to Tasha, but the words would have floated out of me regardless of the audience as I immersed myself in this new revelation. "Strange. Why have I always thought reconciliation was something sweet and gentle?"

Tasha shook her head knowingly. "It ain't easy."

"Hmmm. I've always thought black people were stubborn when they wouldn't come to racial healing classes and when they seemed to avoid conversations about race. Wow." I shook my head as I absorbed this wonder. "I've been so dense!"

Tasha turned to look at me directly, her eyes slightly squinted.

I stood up and stretched, as if trying out new limbs.

Tasha also stood up. "I'm glad we stuck with each other, Heather. You a good friend."

Chad was driving a Matchbox car around the shoulders and head of his playmate, making wonderful motor noises. His new friend laughed jubilantly as he pressed Chad's nose with a muddy finger. At four, they didn't *care* about their differences.

I kissed Steve passionately when he came home from the store. "I'm gonna cook you up some chicken, baby," I told him as I started pulling groceries from the bag.

He raised his eyebrows.

"Oh, yeah." The laughter in me couldn't be contained. "If God wants us to stick around, then we'd better learn how to fit in."

"Daddy," Chad burst out, "we went to Deshawn's house! His mama teached Mommy how to make chicken."

Steve's eyebrows curved even more.

I nodded. "You know what I like about the people around here?"

Steve stared at me.

"Wait. That may be a generalization. Do you know what I like about Dolores so much?"

"Dolores?"

"Deshawn's mom. She forgives so easily. She even gave me some corn bread."

"Corn bread?"

"Yeah." I stopped reaching into the brown bags and looked up at Steve. "Something happened to me today."

"I see."

I grinned widely. "Oh, hey. Do you mind if Deshawn spends more time with us? He's such a sweet boy. And his mom … wow." I looked around at my beautiful family and my cozy home. Dolores's rotting furniture and smoke-filled rooms matched the painful childhood she flippantly revealed to me; her current drug- and boyfriend-related problems happened before my eyes. "Well, I don't know how she survives with the life she has."

He leaned over the counter to kiss me. "I think that would be wonderful."

That week I asked the kids who hung out at our house to help me plant perennials in the black, spring soil—and a new tradition was birthed. They proudly joined me in watering and weeding the flowers rather than plucking them. Cuss words were rare because no one could bear being sent out to watch through the fence all afternoon.

Our family began walking to church on Sunday mornings. By the end of the summer, we were able to greet several neighbors along the way by name. One of them started coming to church with us.

Watching the sunset and greeting our neighbors from the front step became a regular habit.

Bunk beds replaced the twin bed in Chad's room so we could make Deshawn's frequent sleepovers more comfortable.

Pumpkin bread baked from the bright orange vegetable that grew beside my garage was exchanged with neighbors for tips on where to buy the best greens in town and how to fix them.

An afternoon of chatting with Dolores one stormy Saturday led to cornrows in my pin-straight hair. "And you gotta wear tighter pants on that big booty of yours, girl," she told me as I walked out her door. "Oh ho. You just keep them hackles down. I'd give up my own sweet granny for a foundation like that."

Comments on the arrogance of white people bounced off me regularly. I struck back by disparaging the loud level of noise coming from the mouths of black folk. As we criticized each other, our arms held each other's shoulders more tightly and our smiles broadened.

One warm October evening after taking Chad to the playground across the street and chatting with the other moms who congregated there, I walked into the house with a swing to my step. "Oh, Steve. We laughed until our sides ached." I lifted Simon up and gave him a kiss. "It's amazing—I never thought this would happen—but I *like* living here."

Steve nodded. "Yeah. I've been thinking about that. Someone at church asked about the house. He'll be at the council meeting tonight. Shall I tell him we're not selling anymore?" He shrugged his shoulders. "I don't think we can afford to move anyway."

I almost giggled. "I guess we're staying."

When Steve left, I put the boys to bed and dropped into bed myself, exhausted and happy. Everything was lovely. I wouldn't have believed, had I been warned, that my life would be interrupted so grossly in so short a time.

But what seemed like only moments later, the light in my bedroom turned on. I groaned and pulled the blankets over my head. "Turn off the light, Steve." The room went dark again, and I grudgingly opened my eyes and peeked out from the covers.

The man standing in my bedroom was not Steve.

CHAPTER FOUR

THE PAINTING

"You better not
wake your babies.
I don't think you want
them to get hurt."

T hrough the dim light reflecting from the hallway,
I saw your silhouette — and vaguely understood that
a tall, black man with thick arms stood a few feet away.
"Who are you?" I asked sleepily. I might have rolled over
and disappeared back into my dreams, but the ugliness of
your voice ("Don't you worry 'bout dat,") shocked me into
wakefulness. Suddenly, I was not only awake, but keenly
aware.

I sat up quickly, and you yanked a knife out of your
pocket.

"Oh, no," I whispered, holding my hands up toward you
as if sheer willpower would keep you away. "No, don't do
this."

You could have stopped. God carefully paints each detail
of our lives onto a giant canvas with the desire of creating a

beautiful picture, but he lets us determine each stroke of his brush. "Don't do this," I told you. "Let me pray for you." I flung the words at you as you slowly pushed me back down onto the bed. "I can pray for you," I shouted desperately.

You laughed—and the sound was wicked, mocking what could have set you free, reveling in the illusion of power.

Suddenly angry, I sat up and tried to get out of bed. My protest grew louder. "Stop!" I screamed at you. "Go away!"

We wrestled only briefly. You needn't have wrestled at all, for your next words subdued me entirely. "You better not wake your babies. I don't think you want them to get hurt."

The darkness hid your visage from me, and I was glad, for I was spared from looking into the face of evil. I moaned as you shoved me back onto the bed. I sobbed for my children, not knowing if you had hurt them already. I prayed for protection. I begged God to free me.

You chuckled as you sat at the edge of my bed, acting as though you had a right to be there. You touched my hair gently, as if your other hand did not threaten me with a knife. "You gonna like this, baby." Your breath reeked of beer, and your words fell on me like vomit. Slowly, so gently, you pulled the blankets off me and let your free hand roam over my body, over the long, flannel nightgown I wore. At first I resisted your touches by slapping your hands and moving away any way I could, but that only increased your pleasure. "You'll be flying, baby. You never had it so good, baby."

Could you really have believed the words you spoke?

When your fingers found their way under my gown, I felt each touch as deeply as a burning coal against my skin.

"You gonna be begging for more, baby." The hardness of the knife against my neck was barely noticeable against the sick sound of your words. I reflexively jerked away from you and experienced momentary freedom. I nearly escaped from the bed.

And so, in your panic, you lost all pretense of charm. You called me "bitch" and slapped my face. You grabbed me violently and scraped the knife over the flesh on my neck. You swore that I would die if I moved again. You snatched off my panties and yanked my gown up around my neck.

I endured the filth of your mouth on my breasts.

I endured your fingers and tongue penetrating my body.

I endured your sweat dripping on my belly.

Your play with my body finally found satisfaction, and so you moved into the final act. I sensed the change coming and whimpered audibly. I doubt you heard me over the sound of your grunts and heavings.

*P*erhaps the agony would have been too much for me if I hadn't discovered a Place in myself where the Comforter dwelt. I might have screamed and struggled hysterically, driving you to worse measures. I might have mustered up the strength to kill you with your own knife. I might have willed myself to die. Instead, I entered the Place that had been newly revealed to me and leaned into Holy arms. I prayed without words and communed with God. The tears rolled down my face, and my very soul wept, but I was safe. I endured.

I silently called out to the God who lets me face only that

which I can handle. But I wasn't calling out for protection any longer. I wasn't calling out for freedom from your pollution. Instead, I was calling out for salvation—for you. "Forgive him, Lord." The words were not even my own.

Once, for a brief moment, you stopped, and I felt your head turn to look toward my face. Were you responding to the Holy Spirit's prompting to quit and repent of this act, or were you simply looking for the knife you had dropped?

You returned to your perilous quest for power.

You found exhilaration by forcing entry into another soul and didn't know you were actually on a roller coaster ride heading straight into the pit of darkness where you would crash into eternal doom. At the end of your ride, you would experience far worse than rape. I knew even then that you and I, though intertwining our souls in a deeply personal way that would remain forever embedded in our hearts, were as far apart as two humans ever could be. And so my heart mourned for you. "Forgive him. He doesn't know what he is doing." My brother, you should have listened to the prompting.

I didn't come out of the Place until you jerked my arm and told me to get you some money. I got out of bed quickly and pulled my gown over my body, thankful for the privacy.

You cursed, for you had lost the knife.

Oh, how I wish I had been in a frame of mind to protect myself then. I might have seized the moment and run away so you would have had to abandon your quest for the knife. I might have used strength fueled by adrenaline to knock you over or to rush to the phone. I might at least have memorized your appearance to describe you to the police later.

Instead, I sank onto the foot of the bed and put my face in my hands. Reality eluded me. I did not consider that I might be moments from death. I did not consider that my children might be dead already. I did not consider that a rapist walked freely in my home. I knew only that my heart was searching, searching for something that was lost and would never be found.

Awareness faded away.

I did not know that it was your arm that pulled me close. I did not know that it was your voice that soothed me. I did not know that I wept on the shoulder of the one who caused the pain. I knew only that I longed for comfort to replace my brokenness.

I wonder what color God used as he painted on your canvas in those moments of embrace. Did the dark shades of scarlet soften to rose in reflection of your gentleness? Or did he swirl the crimson streaks into an ever-thickening blackness as you sought control of me in yet another way?

We went downstairs after a moment. I no longer felt a protective arm, but a threatening knife. Anxiety enveloped me as we descended the stairs — your giant presence hovering behind me, my mind racing for a way to appease you. We had no cash in the house except some coins in a pottery jar that held various oddments, but I dumped everything out to you as a peace offering. Too late I remembered that Steve's wedding ring nestled among the quarters. He kept it there during the week to avoid shocks in his work as an electrician. You stuffed a handful of the treasure in your pocket, snatched the car keys, and then turned me back toward the stairs.

Not again, my thoughts wailed. Not again!

The stench of your body surrounded me, but the choice was not mine to make. Dread seemed to grow into a tangible force that pushed against me as we ascended, but you shoved me until I collapsed onto the bed. I felt myself sliding back into myself, back to the Place.

"When's your husband coming home?" you asked, your face close to mine in the darkness—and I remembered my desire to survive. Steve! He would save me!

"Soon!" I blurted with renewed hope. "Soon!"

We heard a noise. You covered my mouth and held the knife in front of you, transforming my hope into terror, until the silence proved that Steve had not returned. You would have killed him.

"Go!" I told you with new urgency when you uncovered my mouth. "He'll be home soon. Go." You yanked open dresser drawers until you found some pantyhose. "Go!" I shouted as you jerked me over to my stomach and tied my hands behind my back. "Go! Quickly!"

I held my wrists slightly apart as you bound me. Did you notice my self-protection and allow God to paint with gentle strokes? Or were you simply negligent because of your hurry?

The point of your knife again found the nape of my neck. I heard venom spew out of your mouth, but the slur of drunkenness and rush of passion hid the meaning from me. I remained silent. Your face came closer and you snarled the words again, but I still didn't understand. "I don't know what you're saying," I sobbed as you increased the pressure of the knife to indicate you wanted a response.

This time I heard you: "I'll kill you if you tell anyone 'bout dis."

Understanding was worse than not understanding, for I knew your words to be true. "What do you want me to say?" I whispered—and then you were gone.

*T*he sounds of silence echoed around me as I held my head slightly over the pillow, listening. My temples throbbed. Tension pulled tightly at my scalp. Darkness clawed at me. When I dared to move, I pulled my hands out of their binding and then stopped to listen again. I swung my legs over the edge of the bed and then stopped to listen. I walked cautiously to the door and listened. Finally, I let out my breath.

I rushed to the boys' bedroom, terrified at what I might find.

May God forgive you entirely for what you did to me— I bless you! For you spared my babies.

My babies! *I couldn't stay long at one bedside but rushed back and forth between them, crying, touching the sweet, restful eyes and cheeks and shoulders of my peaceful boys. They were safe.*

Full joy sparred with empty despair.

I stumbled down the stairs, hardly able to see for the tears in my eyes. The back door was wide open. I slammed it shut and locked the deadbolt. I found the phone through my blurred vision and called the church.

Maryann's husband answered the phone. "Byron!" I made no attempt to hide my terror. "I need Steve!" I didn't care that the sobs rose out of me for my friend to hear. He asked no questions, and Steve's voice soon replaced Byron's.

"Steve." I had no words. "Steve ..."

"What's wrong?"

"Come home." My voice shook.

"What happened?"

"I've been ..." My throat ached. "A man came ..."

"Heather ..." His voice weakened. "What happened?"

"Steve," I whispered. "I've been raped."

I cowered in the corner of the kitchen, pressed against the wall, holding the phone to my chest, and didn't move even when I felt Steve take the phone from my hands, even when he rubbed my stiff arms and held my face.

I was empty again.

CHAPTER FIVE

VIOLATED AGAIN

My eyes dared him
to accuse me of
the very thing I accused
myself of: negligence.
It was my fault.

You could not have tied me tight enough to match the prison I created for myself in those moments I cowered in a corner of the kitchen.

I felt Steve's hands on my face and heard his voice trying to call me out of myself, but I stayed where it was safe — deep in my corner, deep in myself. His words were garbled and his touch cold. His image blurred before my eyes, though I shed no tears.

I noticed he was gone when he left my side, for fear suddenly loomed over me. My need to know where he was yanked me from my reverie. I began to feel the cramps in my bent legs and the tightness of my own grip on my arms.

"Steve," I cried softly, desperately. "Where are you?" I loosened the hold I had on myself but dared not move.

Steve rushed into the kitchen. "I'm right here." His voice cracked. "The boys are asleep."

I nodded. His arms held me again.

"Oh, Heather." Steve's face twisted with emotion. His eyes, wide and wet, held me.

Suddenly the doorbell rang—and it seemed to me like a shriek from the bellows of a hellish demon. We had been sitting in full view of the glass front door—exposed. I covered my ears, screaming, running, hiding. Steve's grasp failed, and his call fell into the empty space between us. "Heather—"

I stood with my shoulders pushed against the back door, shaking.

Steve found me and took my hands in his. "I'm going to answer the door. Stay here."

"No!" I whispered the word in terror. "It could be him!"

The porch light was on, and Steve had glanced up before coming to me.

"It's Maryann. She was at church tonight."

I looked suspiciously around the dark entryway. "Turn on the light." I still whispered.

He turned the light on. "See, it's just you and me here." He hushed his voice also. "I'll be right back." He touched my twitching face.

I heard their voices ("Is everything alright?" she asked), and I struggled over what to do. Should I go to Steve? I was terrified without him. Should I reveal myself to Maryann? I cringed at the thought.

But Steve was back before I could decide.

"Heather, I'm calling the police." He held both my hands.

"Police?" I didn't understand.

"Yes. Do you want to get dressed?"

"Dressed?"

"Yes. You should put some clothes on before the police come."

"I should put some clothes on." My words thudded like an abandoned racquetball bouncing to a corner of the court.

"Heather, are you okay?"

"I'm okay." An echo only.

He took my hand and directed me out of the entryway. When we got to the phone, he let go of my hand and gently pushed me on. "Go get dressed."

I looked up the stairs and shuddered. Steve stood by the phone, watching me. "Go." *Go.* I had said that word.

I glanced up and then took a deep breath. The hall light was on, and pictures of Chad and Simon smiled at me. Steve still watched me, but he picked up the phone and waved me away.

Alright. I scrambled up the stairs, using my hands and feet like a young child would. I didn't stop outside my bedroom door, but plunged in and yanked open my closet to grab some jeans and a sweatshirt. I threw my gown and panties on the bed and then stepped into the bathroom to put on the clean clothes.

The shower beckoned me—promising hot, clean water that would wash away the filth that covered me. I touched the faucet but then heard a floorboard creak. I screamed and threw on my clothes. I smashed into Steve in my frantic sprint to the stairs and screamed again. He caught my fist before I swung at him.

"Shhh," he told me gently. "Don't wake the boys."

Better not wake your babies.

A sob caught in my throat.

"Come on," he said as he eased me down the stairs. "They'll be here in a minute."

"Who?"

"The police, Heather. I called the police."

Maybe it was his tone of voice—slightly annoyed, slightly helpless. Whatever it was, I gasped. My vision cleared so that I saw the straight edge of the bookshelf and the fuzz on the couch pillow, but my insight clouded.

"The police?" I stared at him. "Coming here?"

"They might still be able to catch—"

"Oh, no! This place is a mess." I immediately rushed through the living room—tossing newspapers, folding throw blankets, stacking books. "Thank goodness the dishes are done."

"Heather …"

"Grab that teddy bear, would you?"

He picked it up and set it on the couch.

"Listen," he said, "you'll have to talk to—"

"Will you close the door to the laundry room?"

"No."

I looked at him.

"No," he said again. "The house looks fine."

"But—"

"Heather, the police are coming to talk to you about what just happened."

I sat down, a coaster in my hand, and repeated his words: "What just happened …" It wasn't a question, but Steve took it as one.

"Heather! You tell me! What happened?" He nearly shook me.

"Maryann was here." I looked at the blue swirls in the design of the coaster and then shot a look at my husband. "What did you tell her, Steve?" My voice accused him; my heart beat wildly. *I'll kill you if you tell …*

"Nothing!" He sat beside me and took the coaster out of my hand. "I didn't tell her anything."

T he doorbell rang. I stared at my empty hands while Steve went to the door.

The police officer at the door was a man. Of course he was a man. He sounded friendly, almost happy, as he greeted my husband. "Good evening, sir. Are you Steve Gemmen?" He pronounced the "G" soft, as in "German."

Steve must have nodded. I was pulling one of the blankets I had just folded over myself, up to my chin.

"I understand there has been a disturbance here. Could we come in?"

I could feel Steve look at me, but I wouldn't look up.

"Sir?"

"Uh. Yeah. Come in."

The man strolled over to me, and I sensed his confidence without looking at him. I heard a couple other male voices grunt a greeting to my husband.

"Ma'am?"

I wouldn't look up.

He sat down in the blue denim chair across from me. Steve and the others stood by the door.

"I'm Officer Long. May I ask you a few questions?"

I looked at Steve. He walked over and sat down beside me—I would have bolted if he hadn't—and leaned forward in his seat.

Officer Long cleared his throat.

"Pull up a chair," Steve told the other men. The words sounded awkward from him. He wasn't used to playing the host. They pulled chairs from the dining room and made a semi-circle around me.

I was the child at the top of a high diving board with an impatient crowd jostling behind me.

Mine was the face under the lightbulb in the dark, smoke-filled room.

I was the bird flinging myself against the glass, going nowhere.

"Ma'am?"

Steve squeezed my knee through the blanket.

"Mrs. Gemmen, did you experience a crime tonight?"

Steve shifted uneasily.

"Heather." The officer's voice softened just a bit. "You need to answer the question so we can get things in motion as soon as possible. The K-9 unit is waiting outside." He cleared his throat. "Did you experience a crime tonight?"

"Yes," I whispered.

"Were you raped tonight?"

I nodded.

"Do you know who raped you?"

I shook my head.

I heard one of the men stand up to go outside.

"Would you please tell me the events of your evening?"

I glanced up at the three officers surrounding me. Officer Long held a pad of paper in his pudgy fingers, and his blue eyes bored holes in me. The other two sat in disinterested poses— ankle over knee and fingers folded behind head. One of them leaned back so the chair strained on the two back legs.

"I—I can't." I looked at Steve again, searching for some sign that he would save me. Even as I did it, I knew he couldn't help. He wanted me to talk, too—to ease the tension, to explain the impossible, to solve the problem.

"Did the crime happen here?" the officer asked me.

I nodded, but glanced again at the other officers before dropping my eyes back to my hands. One of the men had picked up a picture of our family and was looking at it. The other ran his finger over the grain of the wooden chair where a crack had begun to form.

"Steve," I whispered. They all listened, but I looked only at Steve. "There are too many people here." My whispering felt pathetic, as if I were a small child hiding behind my mother's skirt in a room full of rowdy teenagers. But the alternative was worse.

"Okay, guys," Officer Long said. The guys stood up and moved to the door where they shuffled their feet, looking out the window.

"Did it happen here in the living room?"

I shook my head.

"Where did the rape occur, Heather? Please, help me out here." His tone demanded cooperation.

"Upstairs. In my bedroom."

"Mr. Gemmen, is it okay if we look around a bit?"

Steve told them it was alright, and the two strangers loitering in my living room made their way unescorted into my private rooms, past my sleeping children. They took my panties, my nightgown, my sheets, and my new bedspread. Their fingerprint dusting left grease spots on doorknobs and dresser drawers.

"Now, from the beginning, tell me what happened," Officer Long said.

"A man came and made me have sex with him."

"Did you let him in the house?"

I shot my gaze at him, but saw no battle waiting. Still, I growled. "No." I didn't look away this time. I folded the blanket and swung it over the arm of the couch—and the scared child that had covered me since the attack was put aside.

"So, how did he get in?"

"Maybe through the back door."

"Was it unlocked?" His eyebrows lifted skeptically.

"Yes." I directed all my bitterness toward this officer who seemed to scorn me; my eyes dared him to accuse me of the very thing I accused myself of: negligence. *It was my fault.*

He leaned back in his chair and crossed his fat legs so that his right foot stuck out far in front of him. "What are you folks doing in this neighborhood, anyway?" He shook his head and shooed the question away. "Whatever. Are you in the habit of leaving your door unlocked at night?"

"This neighborhood is our home." I leaned forward as Steve leaned back into the couch.

Officer Long persisted. "Answer the question, please."

I could feel myself starting to shake. "Steve was coming home soon, and I wasn't worried. I don't always lock the door."

"You live on one of the most dangerous streets of the city, and you weren't worried?"

"No. I wasn't." My voice turned defensive. "We have very good neighbors." My voice edged toward offensive.

"Could the man in your bedroom have been one of these neighbors?"

I didn't hesitate to answer the question. "No."

Officer Long leaned further back in his chair, looking too comfortable, and then addressed me again. "Heather, are you sure you do not know the man who came into your bedroom tonight?"

Steve stood up to pace the room.

"I didn't even see his face."

"Please answer the question."

"No! I do not know who it was and I did not want him in my house and I hated every second of his filthy hands on my body!"

"Did you tell him that?"

"Of course! I screamed and hit and told him to leave me alone."

"But he still got what he wanted?"

"He had a knife to my throat, and he threatened to kill my kids if I didn't give him what he wanted!"

Officer Long uncrossed his legs and leaned forward in his chair. I smelled garlic on his breath. "Heather, you are getting upset. Why don't you go get a glass of cold water, and we'll continue this when you have settled down."

"No! Let's get this over with so you can get out of my home."

I looked at Steve to see if I was overreacting, but I couldn't read my husband's expression.

"Alright, then. Why don't you just start from the beginning and tell me what happened."

"Officer—" Steve's intrusion into the conversation surprised me "—my wife called me at church right after the rape. She was clearly traumatized. When I pulled into the driveway, the car door was open and the ignition was on. It looks like the person who was trying to take the car couldn't get it into reverse."

The officer looked at me. "Did you give this man the car keys?"

"He took them. They were sitting on the kitchen table."

"Okay. Tell me what happened. Start at the beginning."

I nearly mocked him for his patronizing repetition. Instead, I crossed my legs and crossed my arms and looked out the window. "I went to bed early—"

"What time?"

"I went to bed around nine o'clock and went straight to sleep. I woke up when someone turned on the light."

"I thought you said you didn't see his face."

"I didn't. I pulled the covers over my head because I thought it was Steve."

"What time was that?"

"I don't know. Maybe it was nine thirty."

Officer Long looked at his watch. "It's past eleven now. How long did he stay?"

I shrugged. "What time did I call you, Steve?"

"Just after ten."

"And the alleged rapist left the premises before you called your husband?"

I narrowed my eyes. "Yes."

"So, he's had about an hour to get away. Why didn't you call the police?"

"I didn't think of it."

"You didn't think to call the police?"

I shook my head. *Why hadn't I called the police?*

Officer Long's eyes rolled upward as he sighed deeply.

"Well, what happened next?"

"I went to bed around nine o'clock and went straight to sleep. I woke up when a man turned on the light." I paused. Officer Long tapped his fingertips on his notepad. His wedding ring was locked in rolls of fat. "He, well, he made it clear what his intentions were."

"The facts, please."

"What else can I say?" I dropped my face into my hands. "He raped me, okay? Do I have to say it?"

"Yes, I'm afraid you do. And you need to tell me everything he did. If we catch this man, we'll throw the book at him for every single little thing he did—if you press charges."

I'll kill you if you tell ...

I said nothing.

"So, when you say *rape,* does that mean he had sexual intercourse with you?"

I nodded. I looked at the blanket but didn't pick it up.

"Did he penetrate your body in any other way?"

I nodded again.

Steve sat down beside me.

"You have to tell me, Mrs. Gemmen." Fingers tapping again.

"Tongue. Fingers. I don't know. I tried not to pay attention."

"How many times?"

I looked at him. He sat on the edge of his chair.

The officers who had been upstairs hustled out the front door with bags in their hands.

"We can charge him for every single entry," said Officer Long.

"I don't know. I don't know, okay!" I looked up at Steve. "Steve! Do I have to—"

I saw fear in my husband's eyes. "No, Heather. You don't have to do this." He held my hand so tightly I thought he would crack my fingers. "Officer, my wife has given her report. Would you please leave us alone now?"

The officer stood up, adjusted his pants on his hips, and put the notepad in his front pocket. "I wish I could say yes, but I'm afraid we're going to have to get your wife to the hospital to get a rape kit together. We'd be happy to escort you folks over there."

"I don't want to go to the hospital, Steve."

"It's your choice, of course, Mrs. Gemmen. But if you want some evidence against this guy, you're gonna have to jump through some hoops."

"What do you want to do, Heather?" Steve asked without looking at the officer.

"I don't know." I wanted to drive far away, find a ritzy hotel where I could soak in a hot, bubbly bath, and forget this night ever happened.

"I think you should go if you can." Steve looked as confused as I felt.

"Okay." I picked up the blanket and covered myself. "What about the kids?"

"Mr. Gemmen, we'd be happy to take your wife to the hospital if you need to stay with the children."

"No!"

"No. We'll find someone to watch them."

Officer Long excused himself. "We'll be right outside if you need us."

Steve went to the phone.

I laid my head against the back of the couch and waited to be told what to do next.

Steve answered the door a little later. I did not listen to the words he exchanged with our friends who had come to pick up Chad and Simon. I did not stand up to accept the hug offered me. I did not kiss my sleeping children good-bye.

I put on my shoes and coat when Steve brought them to me. I walked to the front door.

And then I screamed.

Blue and red lights from a caravan of police units swirled on the walkway; men in uniforms hovered in my yard; crowds of people, including Deshawn's mom and others I knew, hung out on the sidewalk, their shadows looming under the streetlamps.

"I can't." I had retreated to the kitchen. "I can't go past them."

Steve left me standing in the back entryway while he brought the car around to the back door. He drove right up on the grass so I could step from the house to the car. As we pulled out of the driveway, I hid under my coat, clutching Steve's arm in terror.

And, still, the nightmare wasn't over.

CHAPTER SIX

ILLUSIONS LOST

Death does not seem so
gruesome or final
when you are holding it
in your hand in the form
of a tiny, pink pill.

They say that police dogs track the scent of fear. You can't comprehend how satisfying it is to know that you were afraid, that your state of mind was as fragile as mine.

I can't go in, Steve." We were sitting outside the hospital. I watched Officer Long walk toward our car. "And I can't face that cop again."

For a moment Steve looked like he might agree, as if he were flirting with the idea of taking off out of the hospital parking lot and never looking back. But he drew a breath and squeezed my hand. "You'll be okay. I'll stay with you." He opened his door and then walked around to open mine. I took a deep breath as well.

The police officer walked a few paces away as we moved toward the emergency room doors. Before we got to the desk, he told us to sit down. He would check us in. "I recognize the need for discretion, Mrs. Gemmen. But may I inform the hospital staff of your reason for coming here?"

I nodded and walked to a seat in the far corner of the waiting room. I stared at the television show, unmoved by the alligator attacks and beer commercials playing on the screen, unmoved by Steve's arm over my shoulder. Eventually I turned to the people around me.

An Asian woman rocked an infant in her left arm. The baby had on nothing but a disposable diaper.

A wiry Hispanic rose and sat, rose and sat, clenching a fist and throwing stony glances at the front desk. A bandana around his forearm was wet with blood.

A lovely blonde teen wearing white shorts and a white sweater clung to a handsome black man. He wore a hockey jersey and held a towel to his forehead. They whispered together constantly. Once, when her laughter grew too loud, the girl pressed her mouth against his shoulder until she was able to limit the expressions of her love to face-aching smiles.

An elderly white man clutched the cane on his lap, ignoring the flittering attentiveness of his aged wife. Every once in awhile he would push the dentures out of his mouth and move his tongue over his gums. The wife handed him a cup of coffee. "It's hot, honey." The man harrumphed, but the old woman kept right on talking. "Not many people here tonight."

"I'm here." The husband spat the words.

"I thought it would be packed. There just aren't many people here."

"I'm here."

"Amazing. You'd think with a city this size there would be more people in the emergency room."

"I'm here." The old man hadn't moved from his hunched position.

I'm here, too, I silently hollered at her.

I looked at Steve, whose arm still held me. I noticed the lines around his eyes and the stubble on his chin. He no longer looked like the boy I had fallen in love with almost a decade earlier. He looked much stronger now. I leaned against his shoulder, and he rested his head on mine for a moment.

"Heather Gemmen." The nurse's voice surprised me. Steve stood up and waited silently for me to gather my strength. The nurse looked at the floor when we got closer. "Come right in here, dear," she said. "Is this your husband?" Steve eased me toward the open door.

I nodded.

"Do you want him to accompany you?" Her words were hedged in caution.

"Yes." I reached for Steve's hand. "Definitely." I wondered if Steve's mind, as I fled into his guardianship, wandered back to last Saturday when I sat down at the desk declaring that I would be the family bookkeeper now. Or if he remembered my recent bold defense of our female friend who had become a pastor. Or if he thought about how I generally tend to take advantage of his laid-back attitude. I was aware of the change— and I was embarrassed by my desperate dependence on him. But as he supplied all the billing paraphernalia and signed the papers, as he answered preliminary questions and carefully articulated the reason for hospital care, I thankfully retreated into silence. I needed all the energy I had to hold up figurative hands against this unfamiliar emotion, this fear that danced a circle around me, breaking in and moving out again. Its conquest of me had seemed complete only hours before, but I felt the loss of courage too keenly to give up the fight.

Loss of courage. But that wasn't all. Independence! Tenacity! Trust! They had been ripped from me in an act that left no outward scar. They had been my strengths. What was left?

My strengths. When had I ever depended on Steve before? When had I ever grown comfortable in his harborage? I clung to his arm and found a bond. I trusted his protection and found love. Fleeing into the sanctuary of my husband's care did not mean I was giving in to the enemy that crouched at my door.

The doctor will be a little while yet, Heather," the nurse told me as we walked deeper into the hospital. "Let's get a couple of things done first." I sat on the table and Steve stood by the door as she took my temperature and blood pressure. She asked whether I was experiencing pain and if it was okay if a counselor chatted with me for a few minutes. And then she laid a hand on my arm. "Heather," she said, "will you tell me what happened?"

I didn't want to. "A man came into our home …" I paused and looked at Steve for help.

"She was raped," Steve said flatly.

"What exactly did he do, Heather?" The nurse's voice was soft and sweet, but her words burned.

"I don't know. He slapped me."

"Do you have any bruises or cuts?"

"I don't think so."

"What else happened?"

"I don't know. He …" My voice trailed off again.

"She told all this to the police already." Steve's voice cracked.

The nurse turned to him and gently squeezed his arm. "I know, sweetie. I'm sorry we have to do this again." She turned back to me, and I saw a hint of a tear in her eye. Sometimes when I am aware of deep feelings lurking just under my self-control, all it takes is a sympathetic look to transform my courage into pathetic tears. And the more I try to hold back my feelings, the stronger they push to escape. Usually, when I feel this coming on, I'll excuse myself to the ladies' room until I regain my composure. This time, as my emotion tingled under my eyelids, all I could do was let my hair fall over my face to hide my vulnerability.

I watched the nurse's shoes shift in front of me as I whispered the story, in abbreviated form, again.

The nurse tucked my hair behind my ear before she reached for the door. "I've set out a gown for you, Heather. Take your undergarments off and slip into this. The doctor should be coming soon. Meanwhile, I'm going to find a comfortable place for your husband to wait."

We didn't argue, and Steve disappeared behind the closing door. The quiet click snapped the thread that held my security. I was alone.

I wish I could say it was gentle temperament that caused me to resist insisting that my husband stay by my side. If that is what this was, then my "gentleness" is restricted to strangers. I yell at Steve for little things: like starting a load of laundry and forgetting to flip it to the dryer, or ignoring my question in favor of listening to a radio commercial, or neglecting to enforce a rule with one of our kids. I yell at the kids for even smaller things: like leaving toys outside overnight, or crying too long over a stubbed toe, or eating half an apple and throwing the rest away.

It wasn't even fear that kept me from demanding my rights. Fear was why I wanted him to stay. The reason I didn't insist on Steve staying was because I had a warped sense of politeness. Manners had a firm grip on me.

And so, alone and broken in the emergency room, I did what I thought I should do: I folded up my clothes and put on the frail gown. I sat quietly on the examining table with my hands in my lap. Etiquette placed me on the bull's-eye of Fear's assault, and I battled for nearly an hour. Feeling like a child trapped on a bed about which monsters prowled, I believed I would be devoured by despair unless I stayed out of its reach. I remained still and calm, but every once in a while a shiver ran through my body.

"Come in," I yelped in response to the knock at the door.

The face of a black man poked around the door. Thick lips smiled. "Hi! Are you Heather?"

I nodded, and my palms started sweating.

The man stepped fully into the room and turned to close the door. I watched his back, broad and imposing.

"Wait!" a woman's voice called from the hall. "The doctor hasn't seen her yet."

"Oh." The man turned to me and smiled again. "Sorry. I'll catch up with you later." He closed the door behind himself.
I battled for another half-hour.

C ome in," I whispered to the next knock at the door. A middle-aged white man wearing a tie underneath his lab coat entered. He didn't smile, but his face revealed gentleness. He looked tired.

"Hi, Heather," he said as he closed the door. "I'm Dr. Manz. Sorry you had to wait so long."

"That's okay," my manners answered.

He sat down without looking at the folder in his hand. "Are you doing alright?" He was looking for a real answer.

I shrugged. "Do you know where my husband is?" I immediately regretted asking it. I hated revealing insecurity.

The doctor raised his eyebrows. "He must be in the waiting room or the lounge. Do you want him?"

"Yeah, if that's alright."

"Okay. As soon as we finish up here, I'll ask the nurse to get him for you." He took the hammer and checked my reflexes. They were fine. "Are you experiencing any pain, Heather?"

I shook my head.

He placed the stethoscope on my back and asked me to take deep breaths. I did.

"Can you tell me what happened?" I couldn't see his face, but I felt the pressure of his fingers firmly on my left shoulder. I was surprised to discover comfort in his touch.

"Well …" I shivered.

He waited, still touching my back.

"Well, a man came into my home."

Dr. Manz moved the stethoscope over. "Mmm-hmm."

"And he hit me." I crossed my arms to rub my shoulders.

"Take another deep breath, Heather." I took two.

"Excellent," he said.

"He threatened to kill my kids if I moved, so I didn't." Words raced through my mind; I tried in vain to sort out which to let escape.

"Did he have sexual intercourse with you?" Dr. Manz asked patiently.

I nodded.

"Did you agree to have sex with him?"

"No." I shook my head once.

"Then he raped you, Heather." Dr. Manz's words were not brandished like a sword. Rather they were administered like salve over a fiery wound. "It was not your fault."

I heaved one giant sob and then sucked in air.

Dr. Manz strung the stethoscope around his neck and moved in front of me. He looked me straight in the face and said again, "It was not your fault."

"But I didn't lock the door," I whispered. It wasn't my only thought: *I gave in too easily. I let him hold me afterward as I cried. I didn't call the police.*

"Did you invite him in?" He seemed to know the answer already.

"No." So then why did guilt slide its slimy fingers over my neck and into my scalp?

"Well, then." The doctor raised his eyebrows as if to say *I told you so.* I sucked some more air. "So," he said, "what happened? Tell me."

I did. I told the story for the third time that night.

Dr. Manz seemed unaware of time or responsibilities outside this little room. He asked appropriate questions and showed obvious concern. When I came to the end of the story, he whistled between his teeth. "You're a brave woman, Heather." He passed a hand over his eyebrows. "And now, I'm sorry to say, you have to endure just a little bit more. Can you do that?"

"Do what?"

"I need to do a little detective work to see if we can trace this guy. I'm going to call the nurse in to help me. We'll pull a couple of your hairs to compare DNA, and we'll comb your pubic hair to see if he left anything behind. Are you ready?"

I wasn't. "Okay."

The nurse came promptly. The doctor kept talking as he worked.

"Do you remember when your last period was?"

"About two weeks ago."

"You're sure."

"Yes."

"When was the last time you had sexual intercourse before the incident you've reported?"

"I don't know. Within the last week."

"Have you been using contraceptives?"

"No. We've been kind of hoping to get pregnant."

"How about tonight? Did the rapist use a condom?"

"I don't think so."

Dr. Manz took his gloves off, and I tugged the gown around my body. He scribbled out a prescription and handed it to the nurse. She left.

"Okay, we've got a few more issues to look at."

I should have reminded him to call for Steve.

"You may not feel it right now, but you are very lucky that you came out of this in such good condition. I've seen outcomes much worse. I saw it yesterday …" He dropped his gloves in the garbage bin. "But, Heather, it may not be over yet. You might have more to deal with than just rape."

"What do you mean?" My skin crawled—either from hearing the awful word again or in anticipation of his next comment.

"First, you're right in the middle of your menstrual cycle. Pregnancy is a definite possibility."

"No," I said. "I'm having trouble getting pregnant."

"Okay, but we'll still run a pregnancy test."

"Okay."

"Second, you are at risk of acquiring a sexually transmitted disease."

I had no idea how to respond. I wondered why Steve had not insisted on staying with me.

"We'll get some antibiotics that can prevent many problems, but we'll still have to run some tests after today to stay sure that everything is okay. I will have some lab work done on the specimen I retrieved to rule out any immediate problems."

The nurse came in with a tray. Three plastic cups held three little pills.

"Thanks, Betty," Dr. Manz said to the nurse. "I'd also like to order a urine test to rule out preexisting pregnancy. Can you get that started when I'm finished in here? Also, why don't you send this out to the lab and see if they can't get us any answers tonight yet."

Betty took the swabs and left. No one asked for Steve.

Okay." The doctor turned back to me. "I'd like you to take this stuff. Floxin and azithromycin will fight any potential infections." He set two cups on the bedside table and pushed them toward me. "Ovral will prevent pregnancy." He set the third cup on the counter. "Don't take this until we get your pregnancy test results back."

He filled a fourth cup with water and handed it to me. I slugged down the Floxin and the azithromycin in one gulp.

"Okay, let's get that pregnancy test done."

Ten minutes later, fully dressed again, I handed the nurse my urine specimen. "I'd really like to have my husband with me. Could you find him for me?"

"Sure, sweetie. It might take me a bit, but I'll run down to the lounge as soon as I can grab a minute, okay?"

"That would be great." I slunk back into my little room and sat on the table.

Though covered by more than a hospital gown, there on my battlefield, I felt more vulnerable than ever. Fodder had been fed to my opponent; it grew stronger with the knowledge of potential consequences. Time deprived me of sleep, of strength.

C ome in," I said to the knock at the door. It wasn't Steve. "Hi again," said the black man.

"Hi." I shifted my weight on the table.

"I'm T.J. I'm a social worker from the rape crisis center here in town. May I chat with you a bit?"

"Okay." I watched him close the door.

"How you doing?" He held out his hand.

I felt my palm rub against the whiteness of his as he placed his other hand over mine in what I imagine he considered a warm and special shake. "Fine," I answered. "How are you?"

"I'm doing alright." He sat on the stool. "I realize you're going through a tough time."

I barely nodded my head.

"Okay. Well, I want to let you know that you're not alone. There are lots of people out there who want to help you and support you—'cause they've been through this, too."

I nodded. I didn't want to notice his blackness.

"I can't pretend to understand what you're going through, but I can honestly say that my heart breaks for you. This shouldn't have happened."

I nodded. I didn't want to notice his masculinity.

"Anyway, is there anything that you want to talk about right now?"

"No."

He nodded his head and threw a compassionate gaze at me. "Alright. I understand." He nodded some more. "I'm gonna give you my card. You call anytime if you just need to talk, alright?"

"Okay." I took the card.

Steve opened the door.

"Oh, hi," T.J. said. "You must be Steve."

Steve shook his hand but looked at me, concerned.

T.J. looked at me too as he reached for the handle of the open door. "I'll be hanging around these halls for a few more hours yet. Holler if you need me. That goes for either of you." He nodded to Steve and then closed the door behind him.

"Who was that?" Steve asked.

"The social worker." I dropped T.J.'s card in the garbage.

"The social worker!" Steve's voice bounced around the little room. "They gave you a black man for a social worker?"

"Yeah. It's okay, Steve."

"No, it isn't! That's the most ridiculous thing I ever heard. He was in here alone with you?" He knew the answer. Steve wrenched open the door and stormed into the hallway. "Excuse me." His voice was quiet, but his anger was evident. "Can I talk to someone about that—" he paused for a moment "—*idiot* social worker who was just talking to my wife?" Steve's anger scared me. I tried to pull him back into the room, but he ignored me.

The nurse stopped.

"My wife has just been traumatized by a black man, and you send another one in to counsel her?"

"It's okay, Steve," I pleaded.

The nurse looked upset. "I'm sorry, sir. I didn't even think about—"

"I know you didn't!" Steve interrupted. Steve never interrupted people. He turned to me. "I should have been with you."

"That's okay …"

He followed me back into the room. "I should have been with you." He was still angry.

I closed the door on the nurse.

"You're here now." I took his hand. "I'm so glad." I didn't care about being a child.

We waited in silence, leaning into each other.

Dr. Manz knocked before he entered. He introduced himself to Steve and then apologized for the hospital's insensitivity. "We didn't know the race of your wife's attacker, Mr. Gemmen. I hope you can forgive us."

Steve nodded.

"Thank you, sir. We will be more sensitive to this in the future."

I wanted to tell him that we were not racist, but I recognized the absurdity of the statement and so remained silent.

Dr. Manz sat on the stool. "I've got some results for you, Heather. The chlamydia test came back negative. The gonorrhea test came back negative. The syphilis test was nonreactive. That's good news." I nodded in relief. *Good news* were the only words I needed to understand.

"Also," he said, "the pregnancy test was negative." His eyes searched mine. "Do you know what that means?"

"Yeah. I can breathe again."

"No." He shook his head sadly. "It means that before

tonight, you were not pregnant. In other words, before your uninvited visitor came by, your egg was ready and waiting for fertilization."

"Oh." I shuddered. "That's not good."

"No, it's not." Dr. Manz reached for the cup on the counter. "Time to take this."

I held out my hand and he dropped the pill onto it.

"What exactly is Ovral?" I asked.

"Basically, it's a hormone that changes the environment of the uterus so the egg cannot implant."

"The fertilized egg?"

I could feel Steve's eyes on me.

"Ye-es." The doctor held onto the word with expectation. He must have known what I would ask next.

"And isn't that abortion?" Truthfully, I knew the answer. I suppose I was looking for a loophole.

"Well ..." He hesitated. "I think it's more accurate to say you're simply preventing pregnancy. Right now we don't even know if the egg has been fertilized. It's about as early in the game as you can get, Heather. Even if the egg is fertilized, it's only one cell at this point. Better to get rid of it now than later."

"One cell? Where does the DNA come from then?"

"It acquires a full set of DNA from the sperm before the sperm disintegrates."

"Only one cell?" *That's not a baby, is it?* "It must be a big cell."

"The biggest in the body. But it doesn't stay one cell. It divides as it travels toward the uterus. And then it looks for a place to implant so it can continue to divide."

"And then it turns into a baby." My voice betrayed my despair. Could the grime that immersed me yet cling to me, grow in me, reshape me? I ached to feel clean again, to strip off all remains of my trauma. As desperately as I had once longed to be pregnant, I now craved barrenness.

"It doesn't have to." I heard the promise in Dr. Manz's words. The hot tub in a ritzy hotel might not be such a far-out dream. Doctor Manz handed me a cup of water. "Go ahead. Take it."

Death does not seem so gruesome or final when you are holding it in your hand in the form of a tiny pink pill.

"I think I'll wait a minute," I said.

"Take your time. I'll come back in a few." He stood up and held the door handle. "It's the right thing to do." And then he was gone.

I looked at Steve.

"Take it," he said in answer to my silent question.

I wanted to.

"Do you think I should?"

He looked at me as if I were insane. "Yes."

"But it's abortion, Steve."

"That not what the doctor said."

"Yes, he did."

We were quiet for a moment.

"What if you get pregnant?" Steve asked.

I shuddered. "I won't get pregnant." Maybe believing would make it true.

"Still." The edge in his voice surprised me. "Take it anyway."

I was not sure what caused my uncertainty. I was not questioning my beliefs. I did not doubt that taking this pill was abortion, and I did not wonder if abortion in this case was acceptable. I did not waver from my conviction that human life is holy. And yet, I sat in that white, sterile room staring at the pill in my hand with a longing that seared my soul. *I need this pill, God!*

The doctor knocked before opening the door. I don't know how long he was gone. "How are you doing, Heather?"

"I don't think I'll take this." I kept my hand open as I moved it toward him.

He didn't take the pill. He just looked at me.

"Please," I said, my hand swaying before him. "Take it away." If he waited much longer, I thought I would give in.

"Listen,"—he closed my fingers over the pill and gently pushed my hand back—"why don't you keep that for a little while. It will be effective for the next seventy-two hours, and you might change your mind."

It seems possible that I was born with the belief that killing unborn babies is wrong. As a child, I had eaten warm stew from a thermos at many cold and wet Right-to-Life walks and protests. In high school, when hypothetical situations had black-and-white answers, I had discussed long into the night my passionate beliefs on this volatile issue. In college, I earned a perfect A on a paper that lobbied against abortion. And the experience of holding a "fetus" as perfect and beautiful as my other children had clinched my untried conviction.

Integrity is so much more than claiming noble ethics. It is more than holding passionate conviction. Integrity is living out expressed beliefs. It is making choices that accurately reflect core values.

The garbage can was within reach.

I put the pill in my pocket.

CHAPTER SEVEN

KNOWING BETTER

The next person I called was my mother.

Do you have a conscience? Do you ever wake up in a cold sweat at night and wonder what you have done? I do. You have raped, but I attempted murder.

Steve and I talked about my choice on the way home from the hospital. Dawn had not quite crept up on us, and the darkness encouraged softly spoken words. "So, why didn't you take it?"

"Do you think I should have?" I didn't remind him that I had the pill in my pocket.

"Well ..." We were at a traffic light, and the red glare streamed over Steve's face.

"But it's abortion."

"Even if it is, it must be okay in this situation."

I let the words penetrate. "And it's only one little cell," I murmured.

The red light on his face turned green, and the car eased forward. "It would not be good if you got pregnant," he said quietly.

We remained silent the rest of the ride home.

The house was dark and empty. I was glad the kids were gone. They didn't belong in this place. "Do you think the kids will be okay?" I asked.

"You mean, tonight?"

I shrugged.

"Yeah, they'll be okay."

Steve held my hand as we went up the stairs to our bedroom where we both fell asleep with our clothes on.

I woke before Steve did. The sunlight was pouring in the window, shining brilliantly as if nothing evil had happened only a few hours earlier. I took a long, hot shower and dressed into pressed slacks and a soft sweater.

The first thing I noticed downstairs was the empty coin jar. Some of the coins still sat on the table and some had fallen to the floor. I collected what was left and put the jar away. Steve's ring was gone.

I wiped the counters and emptied the dishwasher and tidied the magazines. I opened the windows to let cool air refresh the house. I browsed through my CD collection and played Enya softly. I dusted the furniture in the dining room and living room. I washed the windows.

My house shone, but cleanliness eluded me.

I started upstairs to wake Steve — I needed to talk about what happened. I wanted to lie beside him on the bed and feel his fingers intertwined with mine; I wanted to tell him my feelings and hear his thoughts, to cry and eventually laugh together. But I stopped halfway up the stairs — he had slept only a few hours. I knew Steve needed silence as much as I needed discussion. He needed isolation as much as I needed fellowship. He wouldn't be ready to talk yet anyway, not about something so personal and painful. He would need time, years maybe, to think things through. I did not feel strong enough to endure his silence, his separation from me, so I turned and retreated to the living room.

The pill sat on the kitchen table beside my tea. It insisted on being addressed, but I knew I couldn't address it alone. I picked up the phone and dialed the home number of our pastor. "Hi, Mark. Do you have a minute?"

"I have as many as you need. Lori was just about to send me outside to rake leaves. You called in the nick of time."

I laughed and sat on the edge of the couch. "Actually, I'm looking for someone to rake my leaves. I heard you were volunteering for the job." The easy conversation now counterbalanced the anticipation of the difficult one to come.

"Right. And I heard you were going to preach on Sunday. The sermon title is 'Predestination, Justification, and Sanctification Made Clear.'"

"I could do that." Our laughter cheered me. "Maybe we'll get out of church on time for once."

"*Touché!*" Mark laughed loudly, and I could envision his white teeth flashing through the dark, well-groomed beard. I imagined his pale-blue eyes dancing in his handsome face. "So," he asked after his laughter subsided, "what's up?"

"You know, raking leaves won't be so bad today. It's gorgeous out there."

"True …" Mark chuckled again. "You're up to something, Heather."

I remained silent for a moment, wondering how to break into the next portion of our conversation.

"Hey, Heather." Mark's voice sounded cautious. "Why'd Steve rush out of council meeting last night?"

What could I say? *I'll kill you if you tell …* But I already had.

"Is that what you're calling about?" Mark asked.

"Yeah. I don't know how to say this." I wished we could go back to chitchat.

"Heather, what's wrong?"

For a moment I wondered why I had called. What was I looking for? Mostly I needed someone to cry to; also, I needed advice. "Well, I need to decide whether to take this pill the doctor gave me." I picked it up and looked at it.

"What pill?"

"It's the morning-after pill. To make sure I don't get pregnant."

"I thought you and Steve were trying for another."

"Yeah, but I was raped last night." I resisted saying the words, so they came out garbled. I'm surprised Mark understood them.

"Oh, Heather." His groan was as healing as his previous laughter. "Oh, Heather."

He and Lori came over while Steve was still sleeping. At the door, I started to joke about getting Mark out of his morning chore, but he just pulled me into a hug and held me until I abandoned myself to his intense, genuine compassion. Lori rubbed my back and murmured comforting words.

Unconditional love has always been embarrassing to me. The first time I noticed my reluctance to accept it was when we were newly married, making just enough money to appreciate the luxury of hotdogs in our macaroni and cheese once in a while. My father-in-law slipped twenty dollars into my hand and whispered, "Go out to eat tonight." I couldn't say no, and I couldn't pay him back. I had to smile as graciously as I could, go out to eat, and accept the fact that he did not want me to return the money. This time, broken and scared and confused, someone whom I honored and respected—someone who knew my faults—pushed me beyond my comfort zone of friendly banter into intense, genuine compassion. I needed it desperately, so I accepted this gift I could never pay back. But once I got past the humbling part, I realized that this kind of love was

something I couldn't live without, and I wondered why I had
resisted it for so long.

Mark and Lori's love knocked me into grace. I would have
fallen sooner had I known how soft the landing would be.

E ventually we found our way to the living room, where
I'm sure I forgot to offer coffee.

"So tell me about this pill," Mark prompted.

"Steve wants me to take it."

"But you don't want to?" He seemed surprised. I didn't
blame him.

"It doesn't make sense," I agreed. I didn't expect them to
relate to the bizarre emotions raging through me. I didn't know
how to explain—I didn't know how to understand!—how these
two opposing truths could exist in me simultaneously. "I don't
think I could handle getting pregnant from this—" the very
thought made me nauseous "—but something won't let me take
that stupid pill."

"Is it because you've been praying for a baby for so long?"
Lori asked.

"No, that's not it." I shook my head. "I want a baby with
Steve. I don't want this ..." I dropped my head into my hands.
"It doesn't make sense."

Actually, nothing made sense. It didn't make sense that I
had to make this decision. It didn't make sense that I was sitting
in a sunlit room on a gorgeous fall day, broken and scared. It
didn't make sense that I had been raped.

"Heather," Mark asked, "would you feel comfortable letting
your Bible study group know about this? I'd like to ask them to
pray for you." Lori was in the group. Maryann was in the
group. The other three members were women I had grown to
love and trust as well.

I groaned inwardly. *I'll kill you if you tell ...* had clearly lost the battle, but its power clung to me with surprising tenacity. Of course I wanted the prayers and support and wisdom of my sisters. "Yes," I said in a voice much stronger than my spirit felt. "Please do call them."

Lori used my phone to make arrangements. They all promised to come that afternoon. When Mark and Lori left, I felt a little stronger.

The next person I called was my mother. Steve was still sleeping.

"Hi, Mom," I said as cheerily as I could.

"Heather!" she exclaimed in her soft Dutch accent. "Is anything wrong?" She was three hundred miles away, but I knew exactly where she stood—constrained by the telephone cord— and what her house smelled like and how her dusty blonde hair fell when she put her hand to her head. I wasn't surprised that she asked what was wrong. Still, I rolled my eyes and wanted to say, *Can't I call two days in a row without it being a big deal?* But I couldn't say that because what I would tell her *was* a big deal.

"Is anything wrong?" she asked again with a little too much paranoia in her voice.

I was a teenager again who wanted none of my mother's protection. I wished I hadn't called. But it was a fair question, and it had only one answer. "Well, yeah." I sat down heavily on a kitchen chair and took a sip of my cold tea. "Something's wrong."

"Oh, no!" she cried anxiously. "Did Steve leave you?"

I rolled my eyes again. "No, Mom, Steve didn't leave me. We're happily married. The kids are all fine and nobody died."

"Oh." She must have heard the patronizing ooze in my voice. It wasn't a very good setup for what I was about to say.

"But it is serious." I prepared mental notes for my announcement and tried to leave adolescent behavior behind. "Maybe you should sit down."

"Oh, dear." I'm sure she didn't sit down. In my mind's eye I saw her walking from the kitchen into the hallway, as far as the cord would extend, and back through the kitchen toward the dining room, as far as the cord would extend. Back and forth. She wouldn't sit down in the face of trouble.

"Mom, listen." Hedging wouldn't work with her, so I didn't try. Besides, I wanted to get this out before she accidentally unplugged the phone or clicked it off in her agitation. "I was raped last night."

"No!" I doubt she noticed her own reversion, but she whispered a phrase in Dutch that meant something like *God help us.* I hated making my mom cry.

I told her the dilemma of the pill. It was the only thing I looked forward to in this conversation: getting some commiseration about the difficult decision before me. I thought she might be the only one who would understand the agony of my choice.

Instead I got "Why, take it! Of course!" When I paused she said, "Heather, pregnancy just isn't an option. It would be too much for you."

A part of me gratefully accepted her concern. I nearly swallowed the pill right then as I absorbed the realization of what her statement granted: guiltless freedom.

But another side of me felt threatened by her protective admonition. I knew she didn't want me to suffer any more than I had to. I knew she was willing to give up her own convictions for the sake of my mental health. I knew her mothering was natural and appropriate. But I also longed for someone to agree with my strange aversion to the pill, to make sense of it for me. If this strong woman who had taught me the importance of the sanctity of life didn't get it, then I must be crazy.

The conversation ended with a prayer. It was short, but it was enough. "May God strengthen you, Heather."

"Thanks, Mom. I need to go now."

The last time I heard my mom cry was the day before I got married. I was sitting at the kitchen table arranging flowers, and she was preparing dinner. I was surprised when she started giving me advice on how to make my husband happy; I was even more surprised when I saw her eyes watering. At first I thought it was due to the onions she was slicing. I was embarrassed then, too.

"I love you, *schatje,*" she said.

"I love you, too, Mom. Bye." I turned the phone off and put my head in my arms.

The phone rang a few minutes later, and I thought it would be my mom.

"Hello," I said sullenly.

Only silence answered.

"Hello?"

Nothing.

I slammed down the phone and then ran upstairs to Steve. He was in the shower, so I walked slowly back to the kitchen and glared at the phone until my husband came downstairs.

Steve went to the pantry to grab some cereal and then sat at the table. I didn't really want him to kiss me, but I wondered why he didn't. He started eating without looking at me.

"Look at this stupid pill." I pointed at it without touching it.

He looked up and stopped crunching his Mini Wheats for a moment. I banged the table when I stood up, knocking over the cereal. A bunch of it fell to the floor, but neither of us moved to pick it up. Steve looked at the pill. "Are you going to take it?"

"I don't know," I groused, banging the kettle on the stove. Neither of us said anything until I sat down again, a little more composed. "Mark and Lori came over while you were sleeping. He and my Bible study group are coming over pretty soon to help us decide."

Steve must have noticed my choice of pronoun, but said nothing.

"My mom thinks I should take it."

"She does? What did she say?" I felt a twinge of gratification at his surprise. I was right: She wasn't supposed to want me to take it.

"I don't know ..." I didn't want to talk about it. I didn't want to think about my mom crying to my dad. I didn't want to imagine her breaking the news to my brothers and sister. I should have just kept my mouth shut. I was alive, the kids were alive—life would go on without getting the whole world involved. I turned to the mundane: "Did you call work to say you weren't coming in today?"

"Yeah."

"When are the kids coming home?" I didn't know if I wanted to return to the routine of daily life yet. It seemed both impossible and heavenly.

"We can pick them up anytime. I told them it would probably be after supper."

I took my tea to the living room and watched the leaves blowing around until the doorbell rang. Steve answered the door.

Maryann's eyes were red and swollen. She took Steve by the hand and couldn't say a word. She sat beside me and cried. "I love you, Heather," she finally sputtered.

Each of the women in my Bible study group greeted us in a different way upon entering our home, and each one added her scent to the aroma of love that hovered over us. When Mark and Lori arrived, they embraced Steve with the same concern they had shown me. Somehow, I forgot the looming decision before me and simply rested in their care.

But no decision is still a decision, and so our group eventually stared at the little pink demon on the coffee table and worried together about what to do.

"Is there a real chance you could get pregnant?"

"How does the morning-after pill work?"

"How long do you have to decide?"

Maryann answered most of these questions. Everything she said echoed what Dr. Manz had said the night before. The word "abortion" was not used.

We prayed.

"Father, you promise to give us wisdom when we ask for it."

"Holy Spirit, let us know your will."

"Jesus, we need your comfort, your grace."

I had often spoken similar prayers, but this time I didn't believe any of these words would soothe my pain or ease my decision.

We talked.

"You have to do what your gut is telling you."

"Either decision is okay."

"Think beyond this moment and consider your situation a year from now."

Steve remained silent during this entire exchange. I felt the power of his silence: He wanted me to take the pill.

"Heather," my pastor said softly, "I think you should take the pill." It was the first direct suggestion. I looked up at him, waiting for an explanation. "I'm not sure if this is from God or from my own heart," he said, "but I feel like I need to tell you that nothing will be hurt if you take the pill. I don't think you're pregnant."

His words were true. I knew them to be true. It didn't matter that he had never in my presence resorted to "thus sayeth the Lord" language before. It didn't matter that logic would have directed Mark to suggest dumping the pill if he believed I wasn't pregnant. It didn't matter that I didn't want to take it. His words were true.

The horns and fangs on the pill disappeared. "Okay." I was scared and relieved. "I'll take it."

And I did.
I felt nothing.

"Good," Mark said with finality in his voice. "Now to the next issue."
I dreaded the "next issue," but I listened.
"It's good that we've dealt with the immediate problem, but we need to care for the unseen problem. We need to pray for cleansing for you, Heather—for healing." My friends murmured agreement. I wanted them to go home. "This is going to sound odd," he told us all, "so if any of you are uncomfortable with this, tell me." We nodded. "This is what I suggest: Heather, you go take a shower. We'll stay here and pray for cleansing for you. As the water is washing over you, we will pray that all effects of this trauma will be washed away. Are you comfortable with that?"
Mark's words hit a spot in me that I had been avoiding: I felt dirty. He was right again.
I took the shower, no matter how weird it seemed. That day, singing in the shower took on a whole new meaning.

When peace like a river
attendeth my way,
When sorrows like sea billows roll;
Whatever my lot,
Thou hast taught me to say,
"It is well, it is well
with my soul."

Though Satan should buffet,
though trials should come,
Let this blest assurance control,
that Christ has regarded
my helpless estate,

and has shed His own blood
for my soul.

My sin—oh, the bliss
of this glorious thought:
My sin not in part, but the whole
Is nailed to the cross
and I bear it no more,
Praise the Lord, praise the Lord,
O my soul!

And, Lord, haste the day
when my faith shall be sight,
The clouds be rolled back as a scroll;
the trump shall resound
and the Lord shall descend.
Even so, it is well
with my soul.

It is well with my soul,
It is well, it is well
with my soul.°

Nobody was praying when I came back into the living room.
I wasn't surprised. They never prayed beyond what needed to
be said. Instead, they were laughing. I didn't know the joke, but
I smiled. *I'll kill you if you tell* ... was impotent. The lie had been
exposed.

Before they left, Maryann asked if they could ask others to
pray for us. The answer was not easy. I still hated letting so
many know about this, but I needed support: I still had to tell
my story one more time to the detective who was assigned to
my case. I still had to take the HIV tests. I still had to overcome

the emotional trauma that had been thrown at me. I looked at Steve and he shrugged. So I told her yes.

The house felt strange after they left. I didn't want to read a book or listen to the radio or go for a walk. Everything was clean, so I couldn't do housework. I wasn't ready to get the kids or to talk on the phone. Steve had immersed himself in a magazine and didn't look interested in conversation. I ended up staring out the window again at the red and golden leaves that I had piled up the day before. After a while, I could almost predict where a leaf would land after it was wisped into the air by the unseen breeze.

I didn't recognize their car at first when it pulled into our driveway; I wasn't expecting it. But when Mom stuck her head out before Dad could even park properly, I jumped up and ran to the door.

"Mom!"

"I'm sorry for not calling, Heather. But I had to come."

I sank into her hug without an adolescent thought.

"Heather," she said anxiously, voicing her main concern before we even reached the front porch. "Don't take that pill. I was wrong."

*Horatio G. Spafford, "It Is Well with My Soul."

111

CHAPTER EIGHT

WALKING ON WATER

With the telephone in
one hand and the pepper
spray in the other,
I crept through my home.

Where did you go? Were you watching me during those months afterward? Were you hating me for smiling at my neighbors and laughing with my kids? Were you hungry for the abundance I flaunted? I'll tell you the secret of my strength. And the weakness of my strength.

D id they catch him?" It was the first question I asked the young detective who invited me to sit in the chair on the other side of her desk the day following the assault. Lori had come with me and now waited in the room where "wanted" posters of black men stared from the walls. I was glad that Steve and my parents were at home; I didn't want the memory of this place stuck in their minds.

"No, they didn't," the detective answered. "But maybe you can still help us do that."

"I thought the dogs were tracking him," I said.

"They were. They tracked his scent to a house down the street from you —"

"So they found him?"

"No. Unfortunately, they didn't have a warrant to go into the house. Besides, they weren't sure if he had taken off in a car parked in front of the house or if he had gone inside."

"So when will they get a warrant?"

"They did already. They checked it out this morning. The house was abandoned. No one was there."

"What will we do next?" I asked, as if simply naming the steps could put the rapist behind bars.

"Well, do you think you can describe the suspect to a profile artist?"

I shook my head. "No. I didn't see his face."

"You can't describe him at all?"

"He was taller than me—at least a head taller. He was big. He smelled like beer. I think he was wearing a leather jacket."

"Was he wearing gloves?"

"I don't know. I don't think so."

"All the prints we gathered from your house match your family's prints, except one set that belongs to a child. So that isn't going to help, either. Is there anything else you remember?"

"No." I put my face in my hands and groaned. If assumptions are untried, unproven beliefs, I had one that suddenly exposed itself as pathetically false: Bad guys always get caught. I was shocked to discover that someone who had done such a wicked thing was still running free. "I was such an idiot!" I whispered.

"What do you mean?"

It was hard even to admit. "I covered my face while he was looking for the knife he dropped."

"You passed up a chance to look at him?" I realized that she was disappointed. Solving a case quickly wouldn't have looked bad on her still-green record. "Why?" she asked.

"I don't know. I guess I was being self-protective. If he knew I wouldn't be able to describe him, then maybe he wouldn't kill me. It was dumb." I didn't look at her, but from her silence I guessed she was trying not to swear at me.

A moment later she said my name very quietly and very slowly. "Heather." I looked up at her and saw, if not compassion, kindness. "Let's get one thing straight," she said in a school-teacher voice. "You did nothing wrong. Keeping his face out of your mind might have been the best thing there was to do. Look, you're alive, right?" I nodded reluctantly. "Why don't you tell me what happened," she said. "Maybe some important memory will come back that will help us catch this guy."

I wasn't surprised that she asked this, but I still resisted. "I've told the story so many times already," I explained. "I don't think I can tell it again."

She nodded sympathetically. "It must be hard, but there are reasons to tell. Not only will it help us get this guy off the streets, it will free you up to heal more quickly. You'd be amazed at what a difference it makes just to talk."

The getting-the-guy-off-the-streets argument won me over. The idea of healing more quickly seemed remote, or perhaps unrealistic. But as I talked, my voice shook less than it had the time before, and my heart beat at a normal pace. Detective Boers took meticulous notes and made me repeat things she did not catch the first time or things she wanted clarified. She closed her book at the end of the conversation and leaned back in her chair. "Okay," she said with authority that didn't match her age. "You let me know if anything comes back to you. I'll keep you posted about what's happening on our end. Does that sound good?"

We stood up to shake hands, and then I went back to the small room stacked with metal chairs with plastic seats where Lori waited for me. She was studying the photographs on the wall and reading their descriptions. We walked to the car without saying anything and talked little on the way home.

"Let Mark and me know if you need anything," Lori called after me. "Otherwise, see you at church on Sunday."

S he didn't see me Sunday. Going to church terrified me. "Everybody knows about this," I lamented to Steve on Sunday morning as I flung more and more unfit outfits on the bed. "No one will know what to say. I don't know how I'll be able to look at anyone."

"We can stay home," Steve offered.

"What will my parents think?" I asked. Mom and Dad were downstairs brewing coffee.

"Does it matter what they think?" Steve asked.

I went downstairs. "Mom, I don't really want to go to church today. Would you hate me if I stayed home?"

"Of course not, Heather," my mom answered quickly. "I think we should all stay home today."

"Yeah, I suppose it would be hard for you, too." But I needed affirmation from both of them. "What do you think, Dad? Should I deal with all the questions now, or is it okay to put it off until next week?" If I had asked him whether I should buy a Mac or a PC, or if I should read a certain book, or the best way to wallpaper a room — I would have received an answer that might have convinced even a professional of his expertise on the given subject.

To this question he shook his hand at me as if he were wiping away an awful stain on his windshield. "I don't know, Heather. I don't know." *Don't go* is what I heard. How could I handle church if he couldn't handle even a question about it?

And so we stayed home the first Sunday after the rape. But our absence from church did not stop people from being jarred by the news.

An emergency prayer meeting was called on our behalf. I didn't go, but I was told that Sherman Street's sanctuary was packed. The meeting was an informal mix of prayer and discussion. Pastor Mark allowed people to express their feelings to each other and to God without any expectation that they say the "right thing." Some wept openly. Some admitted their own fear. Some called out for justice. Maryann told me that her husband, Byron, whose anger wouldn't allow him to pray, stomped around the church basement punching things and flinging verbal attacks against the "jackass" who messed with his friend.

Someone bought us the watchdog we had always talked about getting: a beagle whose bite would have tickled a child, but whose bark could rally neighbors a block away.

Someone wrote a newspaper article in my defense against the word "alleged" in the original news report.

Someone anonymously sent us money, lamenting the fact that he or she was not close enough to us to offer emotional support.

Family, too, rallied around us.

A few days after the rape, Steve and I went to his parents' house, where all his siblings had gathered. I was nervous. But when I walked through the door and saw tears on the face of my stoic brother-in-law and felt his protective hug, when Steve and I were sheltered in the embraces of each member of the family, when my mother-in-law looked at me with as much compassion as if I were her own daughter, I wasn't nervous anymore. This was a safe place.

Tasha took over the job of mothering us when my parents had to return home. She accepted the meals people brought to us and answered the phone. (We had received two more anonymous calls, and I hated answering the phone.) She played with the kids when we wanted to be left alone. She brought a large basket from home to hold the cards that overflowed from our mailbox—and she told us to keep these "acknowledgments of love" forever.

Best of all, she trickled wisdom into my empty heart in measures I could handle. Once we were taking a walk through the neighborhood while Steve watched the boys, and she dumped a load of wisdom on me.

"You know, Tasha," I began tentatively. I figured my next words would sound warped if I spoke them out loud, but the thought had wrapped itself around my soul and needed release. "The rape really wasn't a big deal."

"What?" She nearly exploded, but I put my hand on her arm to stop her.

"Just listen," I begged her. "I want you to know that it wasn't so bad. Look, my kids are alive, and I'm alive, and there really are no negative consequences."

"Girl!" She tried to break in again.

"Wait, Tasha. Listen. I'm okay. I don't blame the guy who did this. He's some black guy who has been put in his place all his life by white people. If this is the only payback to whites for how we've mistreated blacks, then it's not bad at all." I was thinking of the time my heart had disintegrated while reading *Aunt Annie.* I couldn't comprehend how anyone could live through the trauma of screaming and grabbing at her three-year-old child through a gate that separated them, desperate not to lose the grip of his fingers, hearing his terrified screams and watching his stricken face, running and stumbling and bawling as the wagon increased the distance between them. And then to hear her master say that the boy would forget her in a couple days. Whites had raped blacks with wickedness that far surpassed the experience forced on me.

I was thinking of my friend—a young, black man—who had been pulled over and frisked too many times simply for being in a neighborhood where he supposedly didn't belong while politely responding to verbal abuse.

I was thinking of my realtor's stories of refusing to show houses to blacks in certain parts of town so that he could keep up his white clientele.

I was thinking of the black kid at my childhood school whom my friends and I had all mocked.

And so I sadly told Tasha, "I don't mind taking this slap in the face as payment for—"

But Tasha shut me up quick. "Girl, that's enough. You ain't no Jesus Christ, so you just get the idea out of your fool head that you can take on the sins of the world. What that creep did to you was wrong. I don't care what kind of hardships he been having and what all them uppity white folk did to him or no such thing like that. He ain't got no right to rape a woman. He done you wrong, and don't let me hear you making no small thing about it again. You hear me?"

I heard her.

"Besides, you just looking for an easy way out of forgiving him. If it weren't so bad, then you don't need to forgive much. He done you wrong, sister. And you need to forgive the whole awful thing."

Who could argue with wisdom like that? And so my warped thinking smoothed itself out, and healthy, painful questions settled in. *What had I lost? Could I forgive?*

A week and a half after the rape, we considered staying home from church again. "No," I said despite the terror wreaking havoc in my belly. "I promised Mark I would say something to the church. I might as well get it over with."

So we went. We arrived a couple minutes late and sat in the back. People looked down when they saw us. I glanced knowingly at Steve.

The familiar routine of the worship service became startlingly foreign to me as I sat there that morning. We sang songs that I had been singing since childhood, and we recited the Apostles' Creed as easily as we would have said the alphabet, but I looked around the sanctuary with the eyes of a stranger. It was expected, but still a surprise, when Mark introduced me. I walked down the aisle and felt every eye on me. I cleared my throat and stared at the notes I had carefully written down. It took all the courage I had to get my voice to speak the words in front of me.

"God knew what he was doing when he formed churches: I don't know how I would have survived the last week or so without the support of this church." I looked at Tasha in the fourth row—her usual seat; she briefly closed a burnt-orange lid over one large eye. "I know you have given this support out of a genuine love and concern for us. But I also know it is healing for you to help us, for each of you have experienced some of the pain that we have. The man who attacked me, attacked also Sherman Street Church."

I hesitated, considering if I should ignore the rest of the words on the page in front of me and find my seat again. I looked up and caught the eye of an older man, one of the first people to welcome me into this church, someone who had often listened to me. He had big ears; they seemed to stick out of the sides of his head—like the character in the *MAD* magazines— bending toward my spoken and unspoken message. He had a faint smile on his lips, as if he were proud of me, and his smile broadened when he caught my eye.

I continued. "Our vision for racial reconciliation and community development has been placed under attack, and I want to be the first to say that we cannot give up. We are far from perfect, and the task before us is difficult and scary, but I know that God can use us to show the world his power and love. All we have to do is love our neighbors as ourselves."

Steve had read my speech in advance and had approved my words. I looked at him now—alone in the pew, staring at the floor—and I wished that he had been willing to come with me to face the church. Even he would have been touched by the scene before me.

The pianist, a lovely woman with long, graying hair—someone who had experienced and shared significant pain of her own—closed her eyes and swayed slightly. She was praying for me, I knew. A college girl who occasionally baby-sat our kids and who usually attended the smaller evening services, wept openly. A young mom whose husband had recently died of cancer held me up with a quick nod of her head. Some close friends of ours, a loving couple who had been married eight years without being able to conceive, held each other's hands and looked ready to spring from their seats to join me if only I said the word. A middle-aged man, a professor of music, touched fingers to his bald forehead, as if he were in pain; he was. A woman whose newborn baby had recently died sat in the front row. She had been to our house numerous times in the last week, delivering food and cards and encouragement.

I saw the newsletter team I met with month after month scattered throughout the pews: a middle-aged single woman whose mischievousness was contagious; an intelligent and warm man who was my age and from my country—a kindred spirit; a high school teacher who kept us laughing. I saw the musicians and readers and actors and dancers I so often consulted as I planned worship services. I saw my children's Sunday school teachers and the parents of the children I taught. I saw the evangelism team that often met at my round table to discuss theology and strategies: a counselor, a widow, a teacher, a mom.

"Even if nothing else good comes from this experience," I concluded with sincerity, "I now know with conviction that God's grace *is* sufficient—and that his church is a family worth being part of."

When I sat down, after walking past all the encouraging smiles and tears and gentle touches, my body trembled.

Abundance: Rich, fervent prayers for me and my family every day. Deep love and concern expressed so freely. Wisdom imparted with such grace.

S o I walked on water: I smiled at my neighbors and laughed with my kids. And I told Steve to go to the next council meeting. "I'll be fine," I insisted.

He didn't go.

But the next month I was still riding the wave of the prayers of my friends. "You might as well go," I told him.

Steve hesitated. We both knew it would be my first time home alone since the attack. "What if you get an anonymous call?"

"I won't answer the phone."

"Can't you find someone to stay with you while I'm gone?"

"I could, but we've got to start to live normally sometime." The anticipation of being home alone matched the anticipation I once had of getting my driver's license: I expected to be liberated. I believed that this action would throw off the last shackle that kept me a victim.

I locked the door behind Steve when he left. I went to the front door to make sure it was locked. Then I went upstairs to give the kids a bath. As they splashed each other, happy and oblivious, I ran downstairs to make sure I had locked the doors properly. I thought about grabbing a cookie—I was starving— but the floor squeaked. I stood motionless, prepared for the worst. Nothing happened. I ran up the stairs to help the kids get ready for bed. We read books for a long time. The phone rang a few times, but I ignored it.

After tucking them in and kissing them goodnight, I knew I had to go downstairs. *I will get something done tonight,* I told myself. Barely out of their room, I froze. *What was that noise?* Long moments passed, and I pressed my back against the wall as I slipped silently down the stairs. I saw the dishes piled in the sink, but the clanking of the glass would stop me from hearing any disruptions, so I left them. The washing machine ran too loud; I turned it off mid-cycle. The radio no longer comforted; I shut it down.

With the telephone in one hand and pepper spray in the other, I crept through my home. When even that activity seemed to echo in my ears, I sat tensely on the couch, listening. Listening. The house did not give up its shuffling noises even when I sat perfectly still. The floorboards seemed to creak around every corner. I wasn't sure if they were noises I simply hadn't noticed before or if they were new noises.

Who should I call? Mark and Lori told me to call anytime. But what would I say? I'm scared? Come baby-sit me? I could call Tasha just to chat—but then I wouldn't be able to hear what was happening in the house. The creaking grew louder.

I couldn't stand it. I rushed upstairs and threw myself into the kids' bedroom. They slept peacefully while I cowered behind their door, staring through the crack at the steps. My stomach felt nauseous.

Someone was in my house! *I know someone is in my house!*

I did it: I dialed 9-1-1.

The telephone rang a few times before a woman's voice answered. I whispered when she prompted me for information. Less than two minutes later, I heard the siren. With the phone and pepper spray still in my hands, I ran downstairs to answer the door.

"Someone is in the house!" I told the officers frantically.

"Okay, ma'am. Why don't you step outside while we do a search."

"My kids! They're sleeping."

"Are they upstairs?"

"Yes."

"Have you checked on them recently?"

"Yes. I was just in their room when you came."

"Okay, we'll have someone stay there with them until everything is clear. You wait on the porch until then."

Five police cars were parked around my house. I stood with

an officer on my porch as two others crept upstairs—guns extended—and two went down to the basement. I saw a couple more slinking around the outside of the house. I trembled as fear turned to relief and as relief turned to shame. The officers found no evidence of a stranger in my house.

No one chastised me for the false alarm. "Sometimes these old houses make some pretty creepy noises if you're not used to it," one kind officer told me.

Even Steve shrugged off my blunder. "No one blames you," he said after the police were gone and we were behind locked doors again—and that after he drove up Neland Avenue toward the flashing red and blue lights distorting our house. I had never seen him move so fast, whipping the car to the side of the road and running up the sidewalk. I had never seen him so scared as he ran toward me and held me tightly in his arms. Still, he didn't blame me.

But I felt sick. I knew I had plunged beneath the waves. "I shouldn't have been afraid," I whimpered.

Steve didn't agree. "That's not true," he said without a hint of irritation. "It wouldn't be normal if you weren't afraid."

But I was hardly listening. I had run to the bathroom to vomit.

CHAPTER NINE

DOOR NUMBER FOUR

I thought about
heartburn.
And throwing up.
And not fitting
in my clothes.
All this for a baby
I didn't want.

I used to wonder if you had been planning that notorious night for years or if your actions were based on impulse. Now I know that how carefully you planned it makes as much difference as how carefully I tried to discern whether or not to swallow that pill.

I missed my period," I told Maryann. "Again." We were sitting in her office: she, with her back to the sturdy oak desk built into the wall-to-wall bookshelves; me, slouched in an oversized chair with my feet on the coffee table between us. We often had our consultations in this room after an exam.

"I'm not surprised," she answered. "Your system is thrown off by the medication and the stress. It's only been a couple months since ..." Her voice trailed off and she looked at me carefully, as if assessing how much I could handle.

"You can say it."

"Listen," continued Maryann. "Ovral works. I'm more worried that you're suppressing your feelings than about you getting pregnant. Nobody is expecting you to keep up this strong exterior, Heather."

I knew what she was talking about. I had learned quickly that people didn't seem content to leave me alone until I had shed a tear for them. And I hated doing that. Strong exterior? I wished I *could* ignore the despair I felt. "Oh, Maryann, are people really saying that? I feel like I'm crying all the time. People are always praying for me, at church and Bible study and on the phone. And every time Steve leaves the house, I have to call someone over to baby-sit me; when I don't, I end up calling 9-1-1. I'm pathetic, Maryann. I wish I *were* strong."

"You are strong. You've made some great decisions. You're still doing the work of twenty people at church—which I don't think you should do, by the way. You seem to be happy. But I am concerned that you're not in touch with your feelings. Take the whole situation with the pill, for example. You had such a strong aversion to the very idea of abortion—even at that early stage, even under those circumstances. I know that's how Christians are 'supposed' to feel, but in this situation it seemed strange to me."

"You thought I was faking it?"

"No. I wondered if you felt so strongly about it because of some situation you've been keeping secret." She looked at me carefully, as if trying to discover something on my face. She must have found only confusion, because I didn't comprehend where she was going. Unless she was accusing me of having an affair and covering it up by crying rape. It was my turn to look at her suspiciously.

She broke the silence: "Okay," she said, "I'm just going to ask you. And I promise I won't judge you."

"What?"

"Did you have an abortion when you were younger? Because if you did, you really should get some counseling for that.

Most women don't understand how traumatizing—"

"No."

"What?"

"No, I didn't have an abortion. You've been the one to confirm every pregnancy I've had."

"Then why were you so opposed to it?"

"Because killing innocent babies is wrong." I might have sounded a little patronizing.

"Is that all?"

"Yes." I didn't mind that she asked me such a personal question. I didn't even mind, too much, that she had considered the idea that I might have had an abortion. What bothered me was her incredulity of my motives: I felt confused enough about my irrational conviction without her doubt on top of it.

"Oh. You're sure you're not suppressing your feelings?"

"I'm sure. Do you want to know how I feel now? Lousy. I think I'm pregnant, and I expect to find out someday that I have AIDS."

She shook her head. "I can't even imagine the depth of your fear. I'd be terrified. But actually, Heather, neither of these situations is likely. Look, you took the Ovral—" she waited for me to acknowledge this, which I finally did with a shrug of my shoulders "—and the first HIV test already came back negative."

"Big deal," I answered with as much enthusiasm as a turkey might muster after being passed over for Thanksgiving in anticipation of Christmas. "I still have twenty tests to go before we know for sure I don't have AIDS."

"Four," she corrected me.

"Okay, four. But waiting two years is going to kill me."

"Yeah," she agreed. "That's going to be tough. By the way, you and Steve are still holding off, right?"

"Yeah. I don't want to have sex anyway."

"Are you talking to your counselor about that? I mean, you

certainly have to wait until the six-month test proves clear—and even after that you should use a condom—but meanwhile you'd better be dealing with your emotions."

I shrugged. My sex drive—or lack of it—was not on my list of concerns. "I feel like I'm pregnant, Maryann."

"Well, you've said that before and you weren't. Sometimes I think you believe you're pregnant so much that your body starts to act like it is."

"I've never had it this bad. I've been eating like crazy and puking."

She sighed. "Would you like to take a test just to be sure?" Her voice was slightly patronizing, but I didn't blame her. I was slightly embarrassed to wonder if I was pregnant. We both knew it was impossible.

"Yeah, I'll take the test," I said. "Maybe then I can quit worrying about it." But I didn't move. I wanted to mope a bit longer. "Who was it who said, 'A woman is like tea; you know what she's made of when she's in hot water'?" I asked morosely.

Maryann stood up. I knew she was holding up other patients for me. "It was Eleanor Roosevelt," she said. "But you quoted her wrong." I grinned and she chuckled, adding, "Besides, you've still got a lot of steeping to do before you'll taste any good."

"Aw, go suck a lemon," I told her.

"Go pee in a cup," she retorted.

I laughed in spite of myself and went to the bathroom. After putting the cup on the little shelf in the wall, I went back to Maryann's office and curled up in the chair. A picture of John Perkins on the cover of a magazine caught my attention. I had heard him speak several times at various conferences. An amazing man. Though harshly beaten and abused just for being black, he still worked tenaciously for

racial peace—and with such grace! His wisdom had clearly
been refined in fires hotter than I had been through. I picked up
the magazine to keep myself occupied while I waited for
Maryann. A paper slid out of the magazine. I was surprised to
see an article I had written for the church newsletter a month
ago—before a stranger invaded my bedroom. I skimmed it and
felt my face grow hot.

> One of the reasons our inner cities are deteriorating
> is because anyone who *can* moves out, leaving behind
> the poor and broken. The only way to heal the inner
> cities is to fill them with people who are willing to
> work for community development, not for just a day
> or a week, but for years of daily living. No matter
> what the consequences.

I was suddenly jealous of the innocent faith I had lost. It
wasn't that I disagreed with the words I had written, it was that
it didn't seem so easy anymore. *No matter what the consequences?* I
thought of Dr. Martin Luther King, Jr., who struggled deeply
with fear, aware of the constant threat on his life. He confessed
to God that he wanted to quit. Still, he walked in step with the
Spirit until God gave him the peace that passes understanding.
And then he was murdered!

No matter what the consequences?

The man pictured on the magazine in my lap didn't seem to
care about the consequences. He faced beatings and imprisonment
to fight for reconciliation. He risked his children's security by
allowing them to integrate a school when tolerance was not an
American value. He persevered in difficult relationships so that
unity could grow.

And my article lauded these men as heroes.

A distinguished professor, who happened to be my cousin

and friend, had scoffed at my article. Always cynical about my living in the city, he tossed it back at me and said, "I don't know why you continue to believe that you or your church will ever succeed in achieving that crazy dream. An inner-city neighborhood cannot be peaceful."

But I had maintained my faith and told him so.

"Listen," he ranted, "if even one person from your church moves into the inner city in support of this vision, I will be very surprised. Perhaps I'll even reconsider faith. But it won't happen. People know deep down that there is no God and therefore there is no worthwhile cause for which to sacrifice so much."

Apparently my choice to live in the city didn't count.

After the rape, his cynicism had turned to anger. "You're not moving?" he raved. "Heather, it's irresponsible to stay. Who knows, next time it may be your kids."

"God can handle things," I told him confidently. I believed it then — I was still riding the wave of the prayers of my friends. But now I squirmed. I hated being afraid.

I stuck the copy of my article between the pages of the magazine and glanced into the hallway. I waved down a nurse I hadn't met before and asked her if she had the results of my test yet. I wanted to get home. She grinned mischievously. "You'll have to wait for Dr. DeHaan," she said, "but I think you're going to like what you hear." She disappeared with a cheery wink before I could ask any questions.

"Great," I muttered to myself.

Eventually Maryann went to the nurses' station. I watched her through the open door. She talked with her employees like she talked with me: straightforward but kind, precise but down-to-earth. She wasn't talking about me, and I didn't pay much attention to what she said. But I watched her expression when the cheery nurse handed her my file.

Maryann glanced at the paper and then immediately flung her wide eyes in my direction.

I swore under my breath and tossed the magazine on the coffee table.

"Heather," she said when she walked in the room a second later. Her voice trembled.

"I don't even want to hear it." I put my fingers in my ears and playfully sang "La, la, la" to drown out her voice.

"This is not a game, Heather," she said when I stopped. She was sitting on the coffee table.

I wanted us to laugh, but we didn't.

"I've changed my mind, Maryann. I don't want to take the test."

She shook her head, ignoring my inappropriate behavior. "The test was positive. I can't believe it's positive."

We were both silent. I thought about heartburn. And throwing up. And not fitting in my clothes. All this for a baby I didn't want.

"You'd better call Steve," she said at last.

I didn't say anything, but I was thinking like mad.

"Heather?"

"I'll bet I have AIDS, too," I finally said.

"Stop it, Heather."

I dropped my face into my hands. I didn't want to laugh anymore. "I can't do this, Maryann."

I felt her hand on my shoulder.

"Mark said I wasn't pregnant," I muttered. As if that accusation could remedy the situation.

"That's not exactly what he said. Anyway, you'll have to talk to Mark about it. Talk to God about it." She waved her hand. "But that's not your immediate concern. Whatever the reason, you are pregnant. You'd better call Steve."

"What am I going to tell him?"

"That you're pregnant."

I groaned. "I can't tell him that."

"You have to."

I held my head as if I could contain the explosion happening inside. "Why didn't the Ovral work?" I asked.

Maryann shook her head. "I don't know. But you're avoiding the issue. Call your husband."

"I know. I will. I'm going home and I'll call from there."

"I'll call Mark for you," she told me. "This is too big for you guys to handle alone."

As soon I got the boys home and occupied I called Steve's cell phone. I rarely called him at the job site, so I didn't need to say, "I've got some bad news." But I did anyway.

I heard him readjust his phone. "What is it?" I'm sure his mind must have gone back to the last time I called him with bad news. I wondered which news would be worse.

"I'm pregnant."

"You're pregnant?"

"Yeah. Maryann gave me a test."

"How can you be?"

"Don't ask me. Maryann told me to take it up with God."

"I'm coming home. I'll be there soon."

I hadn't yet dared to think about what we would do, but Steve launched right into it when he got home. "Did Maryann say anything about abortion?"

"Steve!"

"I'm serious, Heather. Even the most fundamental anti-abortion groups recognize that a situation like this is different."

"What about adoption?" Even as I said it, I knew it wasn't an option. How could I carry a baby, deliver it, and then give it away to someone else to raise? But what other choice was there? Keep it? That would be even harder. How could we raise the baby of the guy who raped me?

I wanted door number four to open up and to hear someone declare a new and better option with as much excitement as Monty Hall announces, "A new car!" But all I heard was my stomach rumbling.

"What are we going to do, Steve?"

"I don't know," he said. It sounded like a strangled cry from someone who was dying. He wrapped his arms around me, and I felt his body jerk with emotion he didn't even know how to feel. "Why is this happening to us?" he said quietly.

I didn't quote the poster I had seen hanging in the nurses' station at Maryann's office: *I know God gives me only what I can handle, but I wish he didn't trust me so much.*

I didn't insist on doing things my way.

I didn't make a dumb joke.

I didn't tell God he had picked the wrong people for this job.

I just cried. And as I held Steve's ringless hand, I knew I loved him. It didn't matter that he was not romantic. It didn't matter that he was not the spiritual leader I had always hoped for. He was my best friend. We were in this together.

And so his next words shocked me: "It's your decision, Heather. I knew that from the moment we sat here with your Bible study group. I'm out of it. But I can't be part of that baby. I just can't. I'm sorry." He got up from the couch and walked to the family room where he slouched between the boys in front of a video.

I called Tasha.
I hardly gave her time to grieve the fact that I was pregnant. "Do you think he would leave me?" I asked.

"He didn't say that."

"Maybe he's scared of saying it straight out because he's so used to being good. What else could he have meant?"

"Forget about Steve for a minute," Tasha told me.

"But—"

"Listen, sister. Do you think God wants you to have an abortion?"

"No. But what else can I do? And I certainly don't want to put my marriage in jeopardy."

"What matters more: keeping things straight with your man or with your God?"

"Yeah, but what about this whole submitting-to-your-husband thing?"

"Interesting that you start caring about that now. No, I'm sorry, Heather. If he wants you to do something against the will of God, I don't call that leadership worth listening to."

"Okay, so you're saying I should lose my marriage to have a baby that was conceived through rape. I don't even want the baby!"

"I'm saying you should obey God. Besides, Steve is too good a man to leave you."

I sobbed. I didn't want to be having a theological discussion on whether wives should submit to husbands. I hated that topic anyway.

"I don't know what to do, Tasha!" I walked to the window in the boys' room and saw Steve pushing the kids on the swings in the backyard. "I don't want to lose him. I don't want to have this baby."

"I think you do know what to do."

She was right, of course. "Sometimes I can't stand you, Tash."

"Girl, you love me. Now go ask your man to pray with you about this. I'll be praying that both of you can hear the voice of God." I agreed with her and was about to say good-bye when she broke in again: "I know this ain't easy, Heather. I'm sorry you have to go through it. You know I love you. I'll love you no matter what you do."

And so I went to join Steve and the boys in the backyard.

"It's Simon's bedtime." I spoke to my husband more carefully than I ever had before. "Do you mind if I put him to bed?"

Simon minded. It took me half an hour to settle him down. Or maybe it took me half an hour to settle myself down. When I finally moved away from his crib, he was already drooling on his bed sheets.

I sat beside Steve on the grass where he was watching Chad play in the sandbox. Steve didn't acknowledge my presence, and I didn't know what to say. He sat with one knee up and a piece of grass in his mouth. I sat with both knees pulled into my chest. Chad often played nicely by himself; I doubt he thought about his parents' quiet presence twenty feet away.

Finally I spoke softly. "I want to do the right thing. Will you pray with me about it?"

Steve didn't respond for several minutes. I had been married to him for nearly a decade but still wasn't used to his silences. Maybe I had spoken too softly and he hadn't heard me. Maybe he was so angry he didn't want to talk to me. Maybe he didn't think prayer would help. The only time we ever prayed together was at the dinner table where we asked God to bless our food. I assumed he had a private prayer life like I had, but I never asked.

He turned his head slowly to look at me before he spoke. I saw anger and scorn in his eyes. I suppose those emotions might not have been directed at me, but I didn't know how to deflect them. "I can't pray right now," he said. He didn't say why, but I didn't dare to press.

"Okay," I said. "I can't either. It was a dumb idea." I had never been so anxious to please. "I'm sorry." I think I was apologizing for mentioning such a crazy idea, but it might have been more: I might have been apologizing for causing us to be in such dire circumstances with no way out. I might have been apologizing for thinking we could ever make a difference in our neighborhood, for not locking the door, for making awful phone calls to him, for hesitating about taking the pill. I might have been apologizing for sitting beside him. I might have been asking him to say it's okay. That everything would be okay. To have him take me in his arms and say he would always be with me, no matter what the consequences.

He looked toward Chad and said, fatalistically, "You're not going to have an abortion, are you?"

"I will." My own words surprised me. "I'll call Maryann and tell her not to tell anyone. I don't want anyone to know." I'd have to call Tasha, too, but I didn't tell Steve that.

He turned his head slowly again, but his expression had changed. I'm not sure if he looked suspicious or concerned or disappointed. "You will?"

"If you promise not to tell anyone."

"Okay." I was about to stand up—to take instant action on my decision—but he grabbed my arm. "Are you sure?"

"No," I said honestly. "But what else can I do?" I shrugged him off and got up.

This time Pastor Mark's car stopped me. He got out of it and walked up the path to the backyard and waved when he saw us. I prayed that he wasn't here for the reason I expected. "Hi," he said. "I couldn't get you by phone. I hope it's okay that I stopped by."

"No problem," Steve said. "What's up?"

Mark looked at him curiously and said, "Maryann told me the news. I thought you could use some encouragement."

CHAPTER TEN

COMPROMISE

"You're due for your three-month HIV test."

Hatred is not a strong enough word to describe what I felt toward you. Loathing. Abhorrence. Repulsion. It came on me in a flash, but it didn't end in one. I stood trapped, condemned, ruined — all because of your few moments of power.

Mark sat down on the grass. I hadn't moved from where I stood except to turn my head toward my husband. Steve remained motionless as well. Chad, however, ran to our pastor and jumped on his back. "Hey, buddy," Mark chuckled.

Steve and I engaged in silent conversation. Steve turned his head to look at me — and saw my despair. He stared mercilessly at me for a moment and then gave in. He waved his hand in resignation and went back to chewing the grass. I let Chad play with Mark for a few more minutes before I offered crackers and a video to my carefree child. He had never sat in front of the tube so much in his life, and he was delighted by this recent change of policy. I held his hand as we walked to the house, and

I tried to listen to his happy chatter about Bambi, but my ears itched to hear the conversation beginning outside. I settled Chad down as quickly as possible.

"What can *I* do?" The resentment I heard in Steve's voice when I stepped outside contrasted with the resignation of his words. "It's her decision."

They both saw me coming. Mark smiled at me but continued talking to Steve. "I would think that this is a decision the two of you will have to make together."

Steve grunted.

"How could it not be, Steve?" Mark pressed. "It affects you as much as Heather."

Steve didn't look up when he answered. "I can't make her do something she doesn't want to do."

I thought he was complaining about my stubbornness, so I blurted, without thinking, "I said I would."

Steve looked up at me and shook his head. "I mean that I can't ask you to do it. I know you don't want to and that ultimately you won't be able to do it. And abortion probably is wrong." He shrugged and then turned to Mark. "But I can't stand to think that she's pregnant from this. I just can't stand it." I knew he felt as trapped as I did.

I was surprised to feel slightly disappointed that he was releasing me from abortion; if he insisted on abortion, my problem would be gone, and I could privately blame the crime on Steve. I shuddered at my wickedness. I wondered at the stability of my mind.

"Have you guys thought about giving the baby up for adoption?" Mark offered tentatively. That was door number two; I wanted door number four.

"I can't do that," I said.

"Do you want to keep the baby?" Mark asked, surprised.

"No. I can't do that, either."

Steve looked irritated. "You have to do something," he said.

I kept looking at Mark. Waiting for another option. We were all silent for a moment.

"Jon and Barb Adams want a baby," Steve mentioned as casually as if he were noting the weather. But the effect was not casual: I was propelled into envisioning the reality of this possibility. I thought of the late-night conversations we had with our friends, agonizing with them over the pain of being barren. They loved children. We loved them for loving our children.

Mark and Steve both watched me as the freedom of choice choked me. I knew I had to do something, but I wanted to stall. "Do I have to decide right now?" I asked. Maybe in time I would feel comfortable with someone else raising the child of my womb. Especially when I knew how terrific the potential parents would be. But not yet.

"Take all the time you need," Mark answered. "This is no small thing."

Steve glowered. I didn't blame him. The answer seemed obvious now.

"I encourage the two of you to talk and pray about this until you both feel comfortable with the decision," Mark told us.

Yeah, right. I thought. *Talk. Pray. Comfortable.* My silent sarcasm was not directed at Mark. And my anger was not directed only at Steve.

But my real anger had no one to receive it. So I turned to Steve when Mark left: "Why don't you just tell me what to do? Don't give me this it's-all-up-to-you crap. We have to decide together." He looked about to say something, but I intercepted his words. "No, I'm not going to have an abortion." Steve looked at me with agonizingly patient eyes. He remained silent, and I recognized the illogic of my outburst. "Oh, be quiet," I told his silence, and stormed into the house.

He didn't follow me immediately, and I was mad about that,

too. When he finally came in the house and tried to kiss me, I shouted at him again. "Leave me alone!" When he left me alone, I cried that he didn't hold me.

It took the rest of the evening and the quietness of the house after the kids were in bed for me to settle down. My anger, like the glowing coals of the sunset, cooled into deep blue sadness and then desperate blackness. So I went quietly to Steve. I sat beside him on the couch and laid my head in his lap. He set down his magazine and stroked my hair. I waited a long time before I spoke. "I can't have an abortion, Steve. But maybe I can give the baby up for adoption."

He said nothing but continued to stroke my hair.

"Maybe it would be good to give the baby to Jon and Barb. What a gift that would be for them."

He remained quiet.

"I don't think I would mind seeing the baby around."

He rubbed my shoulders.

"I know they would be good parents."

I rested on his lap, imagining how happy our friends would be to have a child—an infant. They could come to doctor appointments with me. Maybe they could even be there for the birth. They could name the baby. I pictured the joy on their faces as they embraced a newborn.

Steve picked up the magazine, leaving one hand to rest on my back, but I remained as still as the emotions inside me.

"It's the right thing to do," I finally concluded, as if he had shared in my silent conversation.

But that night I dreamed of nearly dying in childbirth and then not knowing the name or gender of the baby I delivered.

I didn't call Jon and Barb the next day. Or the next week. Neither did I keep the pregnancy a secret. I told people my news as calmly as I told them that Chad had chicken pox. Just one of those things. I was aware that people probably thought I was "suppressing" emotions, to use Maryann's analysis —and maybe this time I was. I certainly didn't want to think about what was happening to my body or how I would deal with the child within. I ignored Maryann's pleas to set up pre-natal visits.

One card I received read, *We're holding out hope that the baby is Steve's.* I had no such hope.

Another card read, *We are delighted that you have decided to keep the child.* I didn't know what we had decided.

I didn't take out the Christmas decorations. Neither did Steve.

Sipping coffee after church one Sunday, someone said to me, "People in this church just tell each other too much. Aren't there any secrets anymore?" Maybe she wanted to offend me since I was not crying on her shoulder about my pain.

Instead, I agreed with her. "Yeah, I shouldn't have told any-one," I said. She looked embarrassed and mumbled something about needing more coffee before she rambled off. I left the kids in the nursery and waited for Steve in the snow-covered car.

Maryann confronted me in Bible study one morning. We were at her house. Christmas music played in the background. Her grand tree was decorated with red and white lights and tiny silk bows. We nibbled home-baked cookies sprinkled with green and red candy. "I can see that you won't take care of yourself, Heather," she said, "but please take care of that baby."

It surprised and scared me how I could jump from flat-line emotions to flaring anger. I wanted to lash out at her, to accuse her of giving me the wrong medicine or of misleading me to believe Ovral could solve all my problems. But then she would do something sick like congratulate me for expressing my feelings. So I shrugged.

"You're due for your three-month HIV test, too," she told me.

I knew that. I didn't have the day circled on my calendar, but I saw it approaching like a steam-engine locomotive chugging toward me on the tracks I was tied to. I shrugged again and let the conversation change its course. At the close of the meeting I told the ladies I needed a little break from the group. "Just meet without me for a while," I told them when they asked why. I gathered up Chad and Simon from the playroom, stuffed them in their snowsuits so their arms stuck out like snowmen's, and squinted my eyes against the glare of the white and shapeless landscape. "See you," I called out calmly as we all disappeared into our Hondas and Volvos and Jeeps. But my anger against Maryann's mothering had already formed a plan.

I dropped the kids off at a sitter later that week and drove the precarious roads to the County Health Department. The bite of the wind chased me into the building I wanted to avoid. Once inside, I pulled off my dress jacket and swung it over my suited sleeve. *No one will look at me with disdain,* I assured myself as I walked briskly to the information desk.

"Where do I go for HIV testing?" I asked as indifferently as possible. Perhaps if I had belted out, "I have confidence in me," like Julie Andrews did in *The Sound of Music,* I would have felt better.

I ignored what the young woman's face revealed and followed her finger to a small room down the hall on the right. I pushed the heavy door open and briefly endured the glances of the constituents. A glass window at the far end of the room separated the clients from the staff. I scribbled my first name on the sign-up sheet and checked the box in front of *HIV Test.* Then I sat in one of the plastic chairs surrounding a television screen bolted to the ceiling; I craned my neck uncomfortably to watch it.

On screen, a terribly sad-looking teenager hung her head

and held her very pregnant stomach. Her face was replaced with the image of a patient dying of AIDS. "This could be you," the unspoken message shouted. "Don't sleep around without protection," the actors told us. "Don't share needles." I consoled myself with arrogant disinterest. I was neither a whore nor a drug addict.

Eventually I dared to look around the room at the whores and drug addicts. They stared at the monitor or buried their heads in magazines. One young mom—she must have been sixteen—slapped her two-year-old's hand every couple minutes and whispered a harsh reprimand. She was lovely, but she looked tired. A man wearing a do-rag was rocking to the rap that beat into his ears, looking nowhere. A woman who looked about my age seemed to be ten months pregnant; she leaned back in the chair and rested her hand on her belly.

I smoothed my suit coat and touched my hair. I was over-dressed and I felt silly.

When my name was called, I thought about bolting; but I stood up with grace and confidence. I breezed toward the waiting nurse, smiling. "Hi," I said to her in the tone of voice I used with my Sunday school students. She brought me to a small room privatized with a curtain.

"Did you get a chance to watch the film, dear?" she said to me in the same patronizing tone I had used on her. I half nodded, half shrugged. "It's okay if you didn't," she said. "I have the same film right here for you to watch if you were distracted out there."

"I watched it," I said quickly.

"Good. I need for you to fill out the little form to be sure you have a proper understanding of HIV." She handed me a multiple-choice test. "If you need to watch the film again to help answer some questions, let me know. Otherwise, just give me a little shout when you're finished."

"Okay." I answered the questions in five minutes. The nurse

sat down, crossed her legs, and held the sheet in front of her so we could both see it. She proceeded to read each question and each answer out loud. She copiously praised me when I got answers right and gently added information when my answers were vague. This went on for five minutes before I finally interrupted. "Excuse me," I said, crossing my manicured nails in front of me. "I think it's wonderful that you educate all your clients so well, but this information just doesn't pertain to me. Could we go ahead and run the test?"

She touched my knee and smiled. "Those statements seem a little inconsistent, dear. You want to be tested for HIV, but how the virus is contracted does not pertain to you?"

I nodded my head. "That's right. My husband is my only sexual partner and I do not do drugs. May we please run the test?"

She raised her eyebrows.

I sighed deeply and looked out the window. "I was raped, okay? Please can we just get this over with?"

She didn't talk until I looked at her again. "I am not here to judge you, dear," she oozed. I knew she didn't believe me. "I am here to help. Now, I am required by the state to go over this quiz with you. We're nearly done, and then I can get the blood test."

I listened sullenly to the rest of her lecture. She maintained her sugar-sweet demeanor.

I signed the papers she handed me. She coolly drew my blood.

"The test results will be available in a week—"

"A week?"

"Yes. Please make an appointment for next Tuesday to get the results."

"Can't I just call?"

"No. It is our policy to share the results with you in person. I recommend that you bring your husband or a good girlfriend. If the results are positive, you'll need some emotional support."

I nodded.

"It's humbling, isn't it—" she said as we both stood up and moved toward the door, "—humbling to know how frail each of us is, no matter who we are."

I walked out of the waiting room, past the whores and drug addicts. The pretty young mom smiled at me. A week later I would be sitting with them again, one of them again, frail with them again.

T hat night I told Steve I had gone for the test. He didn't ask why I hadn't gone to Maryann's office. He did ask me when I planned to talk to the Adamses. When I shrugged, he said, "You can go alone to the County Health Department to get tested for AIDS, but you can't call the Adamses?" I shrugged again. "You can face a church full of people and tell them what happened, but you can't call your best friends?"

When have I ever claimed to be logical? I wanted to say to him.

But the next day I asked Steve to make the call. "Ask them if they're willing to *consider* this," I said. "Don't make anything definite. Who knows if they'll think it's too weird to be friends with the birth mom of their kid. I wouldn't want this to ruin our friendship. And who knows what *we'll* decide."

I listened to Steve's side of the conversation and couldn't tell how Jon responded to his invitation to "talk with you guys about maybe adopting the baby." When I asked him how they sounded, he said, "Probably excited."

Before they came, I cleaned the house with meticulousness. I emptied cupboards and wiped down coasters; I rearranged furniture and washed couch pillows; I aired out bedspreads and organized closets. As I worked, I knew the state of our closets was not an issue to our friends—they had seen our dirty dishes, they had teased me about the mounds of laundry, they had discovered our moldy sour cream. But if the pope were planning to stop by, I would have been no less nervous.

I saw the thrill on Barb's face when she walked in the door—though she tried to subdue it. She looked like I often felt on the racquetball court: Don't show the joy of victory because it is gained at the other person's expense. I saw her controlled elation, and my heart lurched. At that moment, I wanted to give Barb whatever it was that would free her to express the suppressed joy that must have been making her skin itch. I knew her deepest longing, and I had the power to let this dear friend realize her most precious dream. We hugged as if we hadn't seen each other in years, though just the weekend before we had been playing dominoes around their dining room table.

And so I didn't protest when Jon followed our hugs with "Guys, I have no doubt that this is an answer to prayer. You can't imagine how thankful we are for this."

And neither did I amend Steve's reply: "This just might be the answer to both our problems."

My cheeks ached as I smiled my way through the evening. I sat mesmerized, as if I were watching a family of deer frolic in a meadow. For fear of sending the nearly tangible joy that danced in my living room back into hidden places, I dared not speak of my growing awareness of loss.

But, hours later, when the laughter trickled down our front step and disappeared into a warmed-up car, when I pushed the door closed and heard the quiet *poof* of the air settling in the frame, when my strained cheeks were released from contrived happiness—I leaned heavily against the wall beside the front door and gazed out the window.

I saw gorgeous icicles glittering from the porch railings, and I saw my friends' footprints in the newly fallen snow as I stood there willing myself not to cry. And, just as clearly, I saw my child nestling in their arms. I saw my child being carried far away from me.

Emptiness had searched until it found me once again.

CHAPTER ELEVEN

CONNECTION

It was our first real kiss

since the rape.

Pregnancy provided one solace: distraction. You consumed my thoughts no more than a buzzing mosquito would bother a soldier in the midst of battle.

T he simple act of standing, as the red taillights of the Adamses' car disappeared around the corner, overwhelmed me. I sank to the floor.

Steve was walking toward the kitchen with the dishes we had used that night and caught sight of my descent in his peripheral vision. "Past your bedtime, old lady?" he called out to me. "You'd never survive the party next door."

I didn't answer.

"Heather, you okay?" his voice still held a hint of laughter. I heard the clatter of dishes being put in the dishwasher.

I knew my husband had not been so happy since my panicked phone call six months earlier. I looked up and smiled when he came out of the kitchen. It was a weak smile, and Steve saw right through it.

"Oh, babe," he said softly. He came over and sat on the floor beside me. I accepted his strong embrace, trying to be strong myself. "Have I ever told you what an amazing person you are?" he whispered, smiling.

I pushed my face into his chest and thought back to the day I met this good man who was willingly walking this difficult journey with me.

I was a freshman in college. My sophomore suitemate, Bonnie, had just taken me shopping. "You've got this perfect bod, but you hide it under those frumpy clothes," she said one day as I stood in front of the mirror, grumbling about having nothing to wear. "Get your money and come on."

She had a car, so we went to the GAP and Express and then back to our dorm. "Wear the jeans," she said. "I want to show you off."

I felt gorgeous and so laughed loudly all the way over to another dorm where some of Bonnie's friends lived. But I got quiet when I saw the beautiful young man working behind the dorm lobby desk whose huge brown eyes smiled at me.

Bonnie noticed the attraction. "Hey, Steve," she called out to him. "Take care of this little girl while I run up to get a CD from Bob." She squeezed my arm and whispered between her teeth, "Go talk to him. He's really sweet." She disappeared into the stairwell, but stuck her head back out to say with a wink, "She just got new clothes. Don't they look great?"

And so, before he knew my name, Steve had me twirling in front of him, showing off my new outfit. I blushed, and our courtship began.

The conversation that began in the dorm lobby continued long into the night in Bonnie's room. A bunch of us college students sprawled on the floor or on Bonnie's horrible flowered couch, gorging on pizza and pop and philosophical debate.

Bonnie was there and a few of my other friends, but I noticed only Steve. We discussed everything from politics to legalizing drugs to Kierkegaard's view of education. We flirted a bit as Steve tried to convince me (as if I had to decide anytime soon) to remain in the great U.S. of A. after graduation rather than return to my home and native land. We threw food and pillows at each other occasionally, but resisted touching each other.

It was way past curfew when Steve finally stood up to leave. He said good-bye to Bonnie first: "Here comes another great year, Bon. I'm glad to see your excellent taste in friends hasn't diminished." He looked appreciatively at me. "Freshmen aren't usually as sophisticated as this Canuck you've discovered."

He winked at me and left.

"He's in love with you, Heather," Bonnie said.

"No, he's not," I giggled. "Is he?"

"Definitely. All conversations combined, that boy didn't say as much last year as he did tonight in one conversation. He's flipped over you."

The next day there was a note on my door: *I heard you were calling out my name in your sleep. SG*

The day after that we saw each other in the cafeteria, and he asked me out on a date.

Bonnie made me go shopping again. "He's a *junior*, Heather." As if for that reason alone I should give up the rest of my tiny savings. "He's gorgeous." I still hesitated. "It worked last time …" She had a point.

Steve held my hand during the movie, and I enjoyed the way our intertwined fingers communicated. We discovered many affinities during dinner at a quaint diner in Easttown and laughed easily during dessert at an ice cream parlor a few blocks down. Dating wasn't a new thing for me, so when he turned off the car back at my dorm, I knew that he wanted our good-bye to linger. Steaming up car windows was an activity I had often enjoyed in my high school days, so it couldn't have been good Christian purity that made me bolt from that car without even saying good-bye. I ran because I knew that I had found the man I wanted to marry. I was terrified of messing things up.

I called him the next day to thank him for the lovely evening and to apologize for running off so quickly—and he asked me out again.

At the close of our second date, I didn't run.

Steve and I spent all our time together after that. We studied together in my dorm basement where other kids played Ping-Pong or watched TV. We watched quality movies like *Dr. Zhivago*, presented by the Student Activities office, and we stayed for the discussions afterward. We met in the cafeteria for meals and in the library for homework. We went to the on-campus church service every Sunday and drank tea afterward. And we lounged in his apartment where his roommates fought over room temperature and chores and food ownership and television shows.

"I hate math!" I passionately declared one sunny winter day as we walked back from Hieminga Hall after my algebra class. I felt like breaking something. "I just can't do it!" I was used to being able to accomplish whatever I set my mind to.

Steve, the math major, my math tutor, nodded in agreement. "Math is tough."

"What am I going to do when you're gone?" I said with as much accusation in my voice as grief. He had signed up for a semester in Spain long before he had met me, but I still resented his going.

"You'll be done with this class before I leave," he said, pulling me into a sideways hug, "and you won't sign up for another math course as long as you live."

"And you'll write me letters every day and you'll send me pictures of yourself and you'll stay far away from all those gorgeous Spanish girls who will try to convince you to never return home to your one true love."

"Oh, babe," he said with a grin. "Of course I'll send you letters and pictures."

I socked him.

Steve's birthday was two days before he left for Spain. I created a lavish treasure hunt for him—making him retrieve notes from professors he hated and from musty old library books most people didn't even know existed and from cute girls he never dared to talk to—until he finally ended up in our friend's cabin on the river, where I was creating a scintillating dinner.

Steve and I had previously agreed that we wanted to resist "going all the way." We also both knew that if we stayed in the cabin after dinner, our resistance would crumble. "Flee temptation," the Bible says. It doesn't say to merely resist.

But time together was running out. We stayed.

I wonder now how different our lives would have been if we hadn't stayed. I wouldn't have gone through the secret terror of researching cancer and other diseases to try to discover why my breasts hurt so much. I wouldn't have wept at the on-campus med center when the young female doctor, who eventually became my mentor and friend, gently told me I was pregnant. I wouldn't have had to call Steve on the other side of the world to tell him he was going to be a dad. I wouldn't have become engaged over the phone. I wouldn't have had to break my parents' hearts by telling them that their good little girl had messed up. I wouldn't have had to sit in my future in-laws' living room alone and guilty while they tried to balance grace and justice.

But then Steve might have noticed the gorgeous Spanish girls rather than baby strollers. ("I can't believe how many babies there are," he said in a long-distance phone conversation to me. "They're everywhere.") We might never have talked about how many kids we wanted, how we spend our money, how our faith plays out in our lives, what our parenting style should be, what kind of wedding we wanted. We wouldn't have held in our arms the baby—the perfect, gorgeous, beautiful child—who transformed us from careless college students into devoted parents.

And I wouldn't have discovered, as I sat on our living room floor clinging to my husband, how deep love goes when tragedy binds you together.

Y ou looked happy tonight," my husband said. "Aren't you happy?"

I sighed. "I don't know how to feel. I want to help Jon and Barb, and I want our problem to go away. I really thought this would work."

"But you can't do it, can you?"

"I'm sorry for being so mixed up."

"You want to keep the baby, don't you?"

"I don't know." I nodded my head toward the door. "All I know is that when I watched Jon and Barb leave this house, I knew what it felt like to see someone walk off with my baby." I sobbed.

Steve remained silent for a moment, but I felt his strong fingers massaging my neck. "Our baby," Steve said quietly.

I looked up at him.

"It's *our* baby," he said. "If we're keeping it, we have to start talking that way."

"What are you saying?" I asked carefully.

"I was thinking about how much pain came out of this—for you, for me, for others. And then I realized that the baby has nothing to do with the crime. The baby is innocent. Why cause pain for her by taking her away from her mother?"

"Or him."

Steve put his hand on my tummy that was just starting to protrude. "Do you think you can love this baby, Heather?"

I nodded my head. "I think I already do." My hand met his, and I liked how our intertwined fingers communicated. "Can you?" I asked.

"If she's anything like you," Steve said, pulling my lips to his, "then, yes."

It was our first real kiss since the rape, and we were both hungry for it. I welcomed his mouth on mine without thinking of the poisonous touches of my rapist, without mistrusting my husband's intentions, without even worrying about passing on a disease. And Steve welcomed my renewed enthusiasm.

We were just getting to the point of giggles when Simon's shrill cry beckoned. "Ahh," said Steve when I got up to tend to our demanding toddler. "It feels like everything's back to normal."

I grinned because, to me, normalcy was even better than sex.

The next day, Steve called the Adamses. "Uh, Jon," he said reluctantly. I was sitting beside him at the kitchen table, cringing behind my hands. "Listen, have you got a minute?... Actually, that's what I want to talk about. I don't think you should call that adoption lawyer yet.... No. That's not it. Heather and I have been talking. Listen, we've decided to keep the baby.... I know. We shouldn't have—" Steve looked at me and shook his head. It wasn't going well. "I know. We feel awful. But it's the only thing we can do.... Okay. I understand. Please call us when you can."

"Do you think they'll ever forgive us?" I asked when Steve set down the phone.

"I don't know." He looked miserable. Jon was his best friend.

"We didn't mean to hurt them."

"I know. It sure seemed like the right thing to do at the time."

Tough decisions can still feel good when you know you are doing the right thing. We didn't feel good at all: Door number three was ours by default only.

We didn't understand the depth of the blow to our friends

until we found out the next Sunday that Jon and Barb had decided to leave the church. They couldn't bear to be around us; they didn't have the strength to watch us raise the child they had mentally adopted. "It was your church before it was ours," I told Barb in a telephone conversation she didn't want to have. "We'll leave so you can stay."

It was an agonizing offer to make—the people of the church had been our lifeline, and losing them was almost beyond comprehension. But the pain of betrayal we caused our friends was not something to be taken lightly. I wanted to, and couldn't, make amends. Besides, I knew that their current pain needed the body of Christ as much as our recent pain had.

But my offer seemed to make Barb even angrier. "No," she snarled. "You stay. Everyone would be mad at us if we drove you away." Resentment dripped from her voice.

"That's not the way it is, Barb," I answered. But she repelled my words as strongly as one north end of a magnet would repel another. I was sad, remembering a recent Friday evening at their house when they had insisted we take back the money we had dropped on their counter to help cover the pizza bill. I knew that, like that twenty-dollar bill sitting untouched between us, Sherman Street Church would remain ineffective to both of us: Steve and I would have to leave the church along with them.

Pastor Mark did his best to reconcile us, trying desperately to care for both our needs, to keep both families in the church. But it was no use: The Adamses had risked revealing to us their one vulnerable spot, and we had deepened the wound. Only forgiveness could return both families to the fold.

So we left the church.

But the church did not leave us.

Maryann was one of the first to call. "You made a public statement, Heather," she told me angrily.

"You said that this attack was not on you alone, but on the whole church. You'd better not forget that."

"I remember," I told her.

"Then why are you leaving us? You don't have the right to leave the church—and certainly not our Bible study—not after all we've been through together."

"I can't leave?" Her words were rushing into me like helium into a balloon, but she mistook my buoyancy for rebellion.

"No, Heather, you can't. And you certainly can't continue to neglect that baby. You may think that I'm being—"

"Maryann," I interrupted, "I called your office yesterday to make an appointment to see you."

"What?"

"I'll be in first thing next week."

"What?"

"I'm coming for a prenatal visit."

"You're kidding! I mean, I'm glad. How—?"

"We're keeping the baby, you know."

She laughed a little. "Everyone knows, Heather. And we're all proud of you."

"Everyone knows?" A healthy church is like a small town: There are no secrets.

"Of course," said Maryann. "We were all in agony with you as you were deciding. I think you've made a wonderfully brave choice, and I think Jon and Barb will get over it."

"Oh."

"You also need to get the next HIV test done."

"No. I don't know why I did this, but I ended up going to the Health Department for the test. I'm sorry for being so dumb."

Apologies were coming out of me unbeckoned on every front.

"And?" Maryann asked.

"I was supposed to go back to get the results weeks ago."

"You didn't?"

"Oh, Maryann! I just can't get myself to go back."

"I don't blame you. That's a tough thing to do alone. Let's have them forward the results here. Can you come to my office today to sign a release form? We can fax it to them."

She couldn't have known how good it felt for me to be back in her capable hands. "That would be great," I said. "I'll have to come with the kids, though. I won't stay for the answer."

"It'll be fine, Heather. It'll be fine."

I almost believed her.

Tasha was another friend who wouldn't let me escape from the fellowship so easily. "Girl," she told me that same afternoon, "I think you just using those friends of yours as an excuse to get away from the church."

"Why would I want to get away?"

"Because everyone know your story."

"So?"

"So you don't want to deal with it anymore."

"No," I told her. "You're usually right. But not this time. I have to deal with it whether I'm at Sherman Street or not."

"Well, I just hope you all get over this whole thing before the baby is born. You know that the baptism has to be with us. This is everybody's baby."

"Yeah. Besides, if we're not at Sherman Street, how are we going to explain a mixed-race baby?"

"You gonna be explaining that for the rest of your life, girl. But you can hold your head up high when you do. And don't you ever forget that."

Not everyone's opinion was as encouraging as Maryann's and Tasha's, though.

"What if it's a boy?" someone asked me. "He'll grow up to be a black man." The person expressing this profound truth had heard that we had decided to leave the church and wanted to make sure we were okay. She talked more than she listened.

"Jon and Barb would have been wonderful parents," another person commented. "Why'd you change your mind?"

"You know this child will be naughty, Heather. Are you sure you want that responsibility?"

These questions from acquaintances and loved ones baffled me. "Doesn't she realize that she was talking about a baby who is as much a part of me as Chad and Simon are?" I asked Steve after we had tucked the boys in bed and settled in the living room for the evening. "Why does she think this baby will be naughty?"

"It doesn't seem like anyone gets how racist and patronizing and insensitive their words are," he answered. "It makes me wonder what I've said to people before that I shouldn't have."

"Yeah. Well, I'm just glad that I've got Tasha and Maryann to keep me sane," I mused. "I feel bad for you. Who do you go to when your best friend is the very issue you need to talk about?"

Steve nodded. "I could sure use a game of pool with Jon right now," he said.

The telephone interrupted our conversation.

"Heather," said Maryann's gentle voice, "I have the results of your test. I didn't want to wait until tomorrow to call you."

CHAPTER TWELVE

DESTINY

"Do you really
still believe God wanted
us to live here?
So you could get raped?
If that's the case,
then God is a jerk."

Sometimes I wonder if you've ever been caught for some other crime you must have committed. Perhaps you, like I, know what it's like to wait six months to find out whether you're going to be on death row.

I hung up the phone and smiled at my husband. With calm in my voice that didn't betray the whirlwind in my heart, I said, "That was Maryann with good news."

It took Steve a moment to catch on. But when he did, he rushed over and pulled me to his chest. "Oh, Heather! Oh, Heather. Thank God!"

I just laughed. I put my head back and laughed until my stomach hurt. I was free. I was alive. My deepest fear proved void. *Thank God* was not adequate.

Steve laughed with me until our mouths found each other.

"So all our waiting was for nothing!" he murmured happily.

We didn't stop kissing as we moved upstairs. We were like newlyweds who didn't have to wait a moment more.

No toddler's cry, no doctor's orders interrupted our giggles this time.

The memory of beer breath did.

I pulled away from my husband. He opened his eyes, surprised.

"I'm sorry, Steve," I said. I really was sorry. "I want to. I love you. I just can't."

Steve nodded his head and then rolled over to rest beside me. "I understand," he said. He even squeezed my hand. But he couldn't have understood. He had waited without complaint for six months only to find out that he needed to wait longer.

I turned from him and closed my eyes. He got up and went back downstairs.

God, I said silently, *I'm off death row, but I'm not yet free. Please, please make me better.*

I woke up the next morning to the sound of the doorbell. Steve was asleep beside me.

I threw on my housecoat and went downstairs. Deshawn was at the front door with his nose and hands pressed against the glass. I opened the door and glared at him. "It's six thirty in the morning, Deshawn. I told you to wait until eight before you come."

"I don't know how to tell time, and my mom is sleeping."

"Couldn't you just watch TV or something?"

"No. There are people sleeping in the living room. And I'm hungry."

I could feel the freshness of the cool air on my face. The city on a Saturday morning is wonderfully peaceful, especially when compared to the nighttime activities of a few hours earlier. But Deshawn didn't care that the clean, morning air offered to wash away the evils of the night. He just shivered in the cold.

I opened the door wider. "Okay. Come in. You can have

something to eat, but I'm going back to bed. It's too early for a Saturday."

"Thanks, Miss Heather. I'll be real good."

I gave him a quick hug. "Ringing my doorbell at the crack of dawn isn't being good, but I love you anyway. Grab a bowl of cereal and then watch a video until the boys wake up, okay?"

Deshawn headed for the kitchen, and I went back upstairs.

"Who was that?" Steve asked without even raising his head from the pillow.

"Guess." I sank into bed, glad to discover my spot was still warm.

"I thought you told him not to come before eight."

"Well, he's hungry." I pulled the blankets up past my ears.

"No leftover food from the party last night?"

"I doubt it. Not with all those people who had the munchies. Dolores's cupboards are probably cleared out again."

"Stupid."

"She is, yeah. But why should Deshawn have to suffer for it?"

We were quiet for a moment, and I hovered between sleep and consciousness.

"I hate living here," Steve said just before I lost awareness.

"You do?" I managed to say.

Steve lifted his head from the pillow. I didn't open my eyes. "Yes, I do," he said. "We were dumb to stay."

"No, we weren't," I mumbled.

"Yes, we were. I'm sick of having to save kids from the crimes of their parents."

My hand slid to my stomach, and I opened my eyes. "What are you saying?"

"I'm not saying anything except that I hate being kept up late at night by loud music and waking up early in the morning to bratty kids."

"Deshawn's not a brat." I closed my eyes again.

"I don't know why I believed all that God-wants-us-here stuff."

"Because it's true?"

"It's stupid," Steve said. "God doesn't care whether we stay in the neighborhood worrying about community development. He doesn't care about anything we do."

"Oh, brother," I said. "The doorbell wakes you up and suddenly God doesn't exist."

"Well, think about it."

"No. You're acting crazy. Go back to sleep."

I rolled over. Steve sat up.

"I'm not crazy," he said. "Maybe I'm finally sane."

I didn't say anything.

"Heather, think about this for just a minute."

"It's too early, Steve."

"You're so content to just accept all this crap that has been happening to us. Do you really still believe that God wanted us to live here? Why? So you could get raped? If that's the case, then God is a jerk."

I sighed and pulled my pillow up against the headboard so I could sit beside my husband. "Yes, I still believe we are called to live here."

"So, you believe God is a jerk."

"Steve —"

"*I* don't think God is a jerk," Steve said. "I don't think he would cause you to be raped. I think he just doesn't pay much attention to what's going on here on earth."

"So, you're suddenly a deist." I shook my head in amazement. I could hardly believe this conversation was happening. Steve is the rock; I am the bird. He keeps me grounded; I keep him interesting. And now I was the one protecting our traditional faith.

"I'm not 'suddenly a deist.' I'm just trying to make sense of things. Listen, it's a joke when people pray for God to intervene. People ask Jesus for a parking spot. If a spot opens up, they thank Jesus. If it doesn't, they say that Jesus knew they needed the exercise. Really, he just doesn't bother himself with that stuff. God made the world self-sufficient, and then he sat back and let us take care of ourselves."

"Okay. So what about Easter? Did it ever happen?"

"Yes. I think Jesus came to die for us. That's the one thing we couldn't do on our own."

"Are you serious about this, Steve?"

He was quiet.

"If you are, then you're saying that everything that has happened has been for nothing."

I heard a video playing downstairs. I hoped the boys wouldn't wake up.

"Is that the only reason you believe?" Steve challenged. "So that this will have meaning?"

"No. Come on, Steve. You know the answer to that question."

"Well, then, we're back to God as jerk."

"No. We're back to God intended for us to live here, to get over our racism, to get to know our neighbors, to get to know Deshawn, to help make this community a little nicer place to live ..."

"And to be raped."

"I don't think God had anything to do with that part."

"Well, which is it? He's either involved or he's not."

"He's involved up to the point that we let him be. He directs us, but he doesn't force us to do anything. He lets us know what we should do, but we decide whether to do it. And that goes for everyone. God didn't rape me; the guy who raped me raped me."

"You believe that, don't you?" Steve said.

"Of course. It's nothing new. You used to believe it, too."

"I know." Steve sighed deeply. "I still do. But don't you ever wonder if we're wrong?"

I saw my leather-bound Bible on the bedside table with its

torn-up cover and its numerous bookmarks. I thought about how no matter when I read it or where in the Book I start reading, some truth slaps me when I need to be slapped or comforts me when I'm in despair or strengthens me when I want to give up or surprises me when I'm bored. I thought about all the people —from in-laws to best friends to acquaintances—who believed God's promises for us when we couldn't believe ourselves. I thought about the startling beauty of God's grace.

"No, I don't wonder if we're wrong. But I do sometimes wonder if I dare to keep being a Christian," I said.

"What do you mean?"

"Well, I'll bet Satan would do whatever it takes to stop us from doing what God wants us to. So I can't help wondering if something like this will happen again."

Steve nodded. "It could."

"But can we live with that?"

"I don't know. I do know that we'd be kind of stupid to stay in this house if we're going to keep this baby."

"You really want to move?"

"Yeah, I do."

"Me, too," I said with a sigh. "Sometimes I scare myself at how badly I want to leave."

"Really? I didn't think you'd ever want to leave."

"Sometimes I scare myself at how inconsistent I am." I laughed. Steve didn't. "No, I don't want to leave. I love being where I know God wants us to be. I love this house. I love these neighbors. I don't want to leave. No matter what the consequences."

"Well, which is it? Either you want to leave or you don't."

"That's not true. I want both at the same time."

"Well, if we're going to keep this baby, we need more space. I think we should put the house up for sale again."

This time I dared to pursue the greater of the two issues

Steve presented. *"If* we're going to keep this baby? Is there a chance we won't?"

Steve was quiet a moment. He sighed when he finally answered. "We'll keep the baby. We don't really have another choice left."

I pushed my pillow back down and told Steve I was going back to sleep. I was sick of this conversation. "I need to get a few more winks in before I get ready for the party tonight," I said. "You didn't forget about it, did you? Everyone's coming."

"Who's everyone?"

"You know. Byron and Maryann, Pam and Alex, Jeff and Dee, Dirk and Mel. Everyone."

"Not Jon and Barb."

"No. But everyone else. We're having a Saint Patrick's Day party. You have to wear something green." I bunched the pillow around my head and hoped sleep would come back to me before the kids woke up.

"No one will wear green."

I didn't answer, but I wanted to say, *You won't. Everyone else will.*

"So, I think I'll call the realtor today," he said casually.

"I'm sleeping."

Steve got out of bed and went downstairs.

I lay still for a while, and then I felt the baby move. It was the first time I let myself acknowledge the fluttering, but I didn't call Steve. It really was fluttering—it was not just a little arm pressed up against my belly with no way of moving away. It was a living child.

I wish it were dead. I blushed at the thought—even though no one could know what I was thinking. *I wish it were dead and it was Casey fluttering inside me instead.*

But even as I thought it, my hand moved to my belly and I

held my breath so as to keep perfectly still. When I finally dared to breathe again, the fluttering continued. I kept my hand glued to the motion inside me until it stopped several minutes later.

And my fleeting thought of moments before was obliterated.

"Good morning, darling," I whispered. I got out of bed and dug in the back of my closet until I found my maternity clothes.

"You look great," Steve said when I came downstairs with Simon in tow. I was probably glowing. "I was wondering when you would give up trying to fit in your other clothes." He winked at me, and I smiled back.

As I cleaned the house and cooked up corned beef and sauerkraut for everyone else—plus all the edible food for me—I occasionally glanced in the mirror to look at my expanding profile or rested my hand on my rounding stomach.

It took most of the day to prepare for the party while also caring for the kids and getting a bit of laundry done. A half hour before everyone was to arrive, I rushed upstairs to get myself cleaned up.

"What should I wear?" I asked Steve.

"Green," he said as he pulled a black turtleneck over his head.

"It felt kind of good to wear maternity clothes today, but I don't know if I want to wear them when everyone's here."

"Do you have any green maternity clothes?"

"Yeah," I held up a forest green blouse. "But should I wear it?"

"I hate to break it to you, babe," my husband said as he brushed a kiss over my cheek, "but you ain't getting any skinnier. You'd better wear it."

I held the shirt in front of me. "But it would be so … I don't know … bold."

Steve raised his eyebrows but didn't comment.

"I mean," I tried to explain, "it would be sort of like telling everyone I'm glad to be pregnant."

"Or that you're getting too big for normal clothes," my logical husband answered.

The phone rang and I dropped the blouse over my head. "I'm going to wear it," I said with conviction as I headed for the phone.

It was Tasha.

"Oh, Tash! I'm glad it's you," I blurted. "Guess what! I'm going to wear maternity clothes tonight!"

I don't know why I thought she would instantly understand the symbolism of my announcement. Neither do I understand why I didn't stop to listen to her before I spouted my own news. She answered with some polite acknowledgment and then I continued.

"Listen, Tash. I can't talk right now because some friends are coming over in a few minutes, and I look horrible. I need to do my hair and makeup. Can I call you tomorrow?"

I hardly noticed the pause between us, and I hung up the phone mere seconds after she told me, "Yeah, that'd be fine."

I wore my green blouse with pride and talked about heartburn and babies with my other girlfriends most of the night.

"It's good to see you so happy, Heather," Maryann whispered to me when we happened to have the kitchen to ourselves.

"It's good to be happy," I told her. "I just hope nobody is mad at me for being in love with this baby."

"Why would they be?"

"I don't know. Sometimes it seems like people think I should be depressed. Maybe if they hear me getting all excited about having this baby, they'll think I'm not taking seriously what happened."

"Nah. You're reading into things too much."

"Maybe." I shrugged and grabbed a bowl of pretzels that had been dipped in green-colored chocolate. "But even if it's true, I don't care. There is no way I want to stay in a place of despair. What's the point? I like being happy better."

"I agree."

I paused outside the door. "I have to admit, though, that a little bit of me worries that being happy about the baby minimizes the pain of what I went through." I looked at my friend's face to see how she would respond to that.

She looked vindicated. "Aha!" she said. "See, you're projecting your feelings onto everyone else. No one wants you to be depressed. You're doing it to yourself."

"Maybe. Or maybe it's a little bit of both. Either way, I'm not giving in to it. I have so many good things in my life. I'm going to enjoy it all."

"Me, too. Now give me one of those pretzels before everyone else devours them."

The next day after lunch, I called Tasha. I wanted to ask how the service at Sherman Street had been that morning and to tell her how frustrated I was that we couldn't find another church we liked. She picked up on the last ring.

"Heather, listen," she said in response to my initial greeting. "I don't feel like talking to you."

"What's wrong?" I didn't notice the emphasis on her last two words.

"What's wrong? Girl, don't you know?"

"No, what is it?"

"Heather, you don't need me."

I started to notice a coldness on my neck. "What do you mean?"

"Girl, you so into your white friends. You drop me as soon as they come in the picture."

"I do not!"

"Yeah, you do. And it hurts. I'm not going to let you hurt me anymore."

"Tasha, last night's phone call was just at a bad time."

"Think about it, Heather." She didn't have to tell me that—my mind was racing. "Personally, I've thought about it enough. And I've decided that it's time for us to part ways. At least for a while."

I didn't say anything. The coldness that had settled on my neck was moving deep into my bones. *Part ways?*

"Good-bye, Heather."

"Tasha, wait—"

But she was gone.

I didn't hang up the phone until the silence turned to beeping and the beeping to silence again.

After some time had passed, I wandered outside to where Steve was playing catch with the boys. Simon giggled with two-year-old glee when I joined the game, and I welcomed his affection with renewed appreciation. When the sun started to sink and the boys got chilly, we moved back indoors where blocks and Legos consumed them.

"Don't ever leave me, okay?" I said quietly to my husband who was deep into a golf magazine.

"I've never even considered it," he said without looking up.

I cuddled up to him without saying anything. He kept reading.

He made it through about four more pages before I talked again. "How can I handle big things when I'm such a pathetic baby over smaller things?"

"Hmmm?"

I knew he wanted to keep reading. I restrained myself for a few more pages until I finally had to say, "Actually, I don't think rejection is a small thing."

Steve turned the page.

"Tasha told me she wants to 'part ways.'" A tear escaped.

Steve looked at me.

"She says that I drop her whenever my other friends come around."

"That's not true. Anyone can see that you like Tasha better than them." He looked back down at the magazine.

I shrugged. "In some ways. Really, I like her different than I like them."

"Maybe she can tell it's different and that's why she's offended."

"It's different just because they're part of a big group. They're *our* friends. Tasha's *my* friend."

"That's what I mean. She's your best friend. Don't worry. She'll get over it."

Steve went back to reading. I went back to thinking.

"No," I finally said. Steve had probably already forgotten what we were talking about. "Maybe I do pay too much attention to them. I really do love Tasha best, but I have more fun with them. And I never invite her to join our parties."

"Mm."

"And maybe I take too much from her. I talk about me all the time, and I never listen to her."

"Mm."

"She said I'm racist."

"She did?"

"Well, she said I care about my white friends more than her."

Steve finally put down his magazine. "Oh, brother. I didn't think Tasha would ever use the racism line."

"What do you mean?"

"I don't know. It just seems like white people can't do anything right. No matter what we do, it's because we're white and we don't understand what it's like to be black. I didn't think Tasha would ever believe that junk."

"In some ways it's true."

"Okay. It's true that we don't know what it's like to be black, but that doesn't mean our every motive is to demean black people. I don't even think about whether people are black or white when I'm talking to them."

"We're supposed to notice. If we don't see color, we're not valuing them for who they are."

"Supposed to. What bull. Listen, I don't want to waste my life in the ghetto when the game we're playing is meaningless. We're not helping anyone by living here."

I didn't know what to say. His logic made sense, but it still felt wrong. "I don't know how we're helping, but for some reason God wanted us to live here."

"Wanted."

"And wants."

"It's meaningless, Heather. And we're both scared here."

It was true. Steve was as jumpy as I was, especially at night. And every time the phone rang.

"Remember," I said, "they might have caught the guy. Detective Boers said she would call this weekend to confirm."

"I doubt they caught him. They couldn't even trace those phone calls. And even if it is him, would you stop being scared?"

I shrugged. "It would help." We were silent for a moment. "Okay, maybe it wouldn't help," I admitted. "A part of me would still worry that someone else would do the same thing. But even now, with him still out there, I'm not really afraid."

Steve looked at me skeptically.

"Really. I'm jumpy. I'm cautious. And I definitely don't want anyone to break into our house again. But when it comes down to it, I'm sure we're going to be okay."

"I'm not buying it. This morning you were worrying that the results of the test were wrong. You're still scared about a lot of things."

"Oh, I was just being stupid. I know the tests are fine. But even if I had AIDS, I think we would be okay."

"Having AIDS would not be okay."

"Think about it, Steve: Walking with God with AIDS is better than walking away from God healthy. God wants us here and so we're going to be okay. I believe that with my entire self … except when I'm being stupid like I was this morning."

No one said anything for a moment.

"And I still don't want AIDS," I said quietly. "God, did you hear that? I don't want AIDS!"

The phone rang. I jumped up to answer it. "I'll get it. Can you put the boys to bed?"

I heard the kids squealing with delight as Steve began the bedtime ritual—which I hated but had to admit worked—of chasing the boys up to their rooms.

"I hope it's okay I'm calling on the weekend," Detective Boers said to me. "I have news."

"Of course it's okay." I twirled my hair nervously.

"Listen, it wasn't him," she said. "The DNA didn't match."

I didn't say anything. I didn't dare use my voice. And I didn't know how to feel: disappointed or relieved.

"Sorry, Heather. We'll keep trying."

"That's okay." I was glad my voice wasn't quavering. "I guess I'm not surprised. Thanks for checking anyway."

After I hung up the phone, I sat on the couch and waited for Steve to come downstairs. A few minutes later I got up, not to call Tasha with the news, but to adjust the curtain I had recently made for the bay window. I wanted to be sure it was tightly closed.

"It wasn't him," I said to Steve before he sat down a little while later. "The DNA didn't match."

Steve shook his head. "We're out of here, Heather," he said quietly.

"Why, Steve?" I whispered in sudden anger, careful not to bother the kids. "Why do we have to leave? I'm the one who just lost a best friend. I'm the one who was raped. If anyone wanted to run from here, it should be me. Why—"

"It's not all about you, Heather. This has been hard for me, too." Steve's voice was quiet, but the tension between us was loud and clear.

"Of course it has. But I still don't see why you have to give up on this neighborhood. We belong here. We're part of the neighborhood. And that doesn't come after just a few weeks of living here. We've invested ourselves. And it's paid off. There are people here who love us and count on us."

"We would have the same thing in another neighborhood. Why not invest ourselves where we're safe?"

I flung my hands up in the air. "Because this is where we've been called! I'm so sick of this fight." I didn't say the next words that flitted through my mind: *Why don't you just go and I'll stay.*

Steve didn't say what was going on in his mind, either. And neither of us looked at the other.

I was surprised to feel Steve's fingers on my shoulders a few moments later. He pulled my hair into a ponytail and kissed my neck. "I love you, babe," he said.

I turned and looked at him.

"I love you even when you're mad," he said.

He kissed my fingers. I offered a doubtful look.

"I love you even when you're right," he said.

He kissed my eyelids.

I held up a hand in mock disinterest, but I had already forgiven him for all his real and imagined faults.

"I love you madly, Heather," Steve said with an unusually playful smile. He kissed my arm again and again, moving his mouth closer to my neck. "You make me come alive."

I finally laughed out loud and returned his embrace. "I love you, too, crazy man."

This time there was no memory of beer breath to stop the expression of love between us. We were one again. I fell asleep in my bed that night safe in my husband's arms, thinking of nothing but this incredible man who loved me despite every-thing.

When I woke a few hours later, I smiled on the way to the bathroom.

But my smile faded when I discovered blood staining my legs and panties. I instinctively put my hand on my stomach; I felt no movement.

"Steve," I called weakly from the bathroom, "something's wrong." And then I whispered to myself, "Something's wrong again."

CHAPTER THIRTEEN

BABY

"We're not going
to lose our baby,"
Steve said again.
And then he went
down on his knees
and put both hands
on my stomach.
"We're right here,
Baby," he said. "You're
going to be okay."

Faith is a journey, but there are definite moments along the way when truth propels a person from one state of being to another. I can name several defining moments in my life. I wonder if you can do the same.

Is this normal?" Steve whispered frantically in the bathroom with midnight silence all around us.

"No." I shook my head. "No, I don't think so." We stared at each other for a moment. I thought about Casey's perfect little fingers that had rested on mine. "What if we lose the baby?" I croaked. I thought of a foster brother I had so many years ago. He was black, and I used to love to run my fingers through his hair. I thought of the little yellow pajamas I had seen at the store the other day, and I imagined how stunning they would look against the skin of my olive-skinned child. I thought of the fluttering against my belly only the day before.

Steve took my hands in his. "That's not going to happen." He brushed my cheek as he put a lock of hair behind my ear.

"We're not going to lose this baby, okay?"

I nodded. "Okay."

"We're not going to lose *our* baby," Steve said again. And then he went down on his knees and put both hands on my stomach. "We're right here, Baby," he said. "You're going to be okay."

I laughed through my tears. "I'm glad you say so, but I'd really rather hear those words from Maryann." I squeezed his hand and added, "I really don't want to lose this baby."

"You'd better go to the ER," Maryann advised over the phone a few minutes later. "Everything is probably okay, but I'd feel more comfortable if you had things checked out. Call me as soon as you find anything out."

On the way to the hospital, after Steve's parents arrived to watch the kids, Steve and I talked about what name to give our baby.

"Let's name her Andrea," I said.

"It's going to be a boy," Steve said. "But I don't think there are any good boy names left."

"How about Ollie after my dad?"

"How about Harvis after mine?"

We both laughed.

"If it's a girl, let's name her Willie after my mom," I said.

"No, let's name her Eunice after mine."

We laughed again and then rested in the silence.

"Are you scared?" Steve asked.

"Yeah."

"So am I. But you know what's really cool?"

"What?"

"It's cool to know that this baby is ours. It's cool to know that I don't want to lose this baby as much as I didn't want to lose Casey."

"It doesn't feel very cool to me." Knowing how much I loved the child within me was wonderful; knowing the child might die was not.

"It's going to be okay, Heather. I really believe that."

I let him hold the hope.

Steve dropped me off by the emergency room entrance, promising to catch up with me in a second. It was not the same hospital we had been at six months earlier. Neither of us had talked about it, but we both knew we would never go there again. This hospital was smaller, but it held no memories. I gave the facts to the triage nurse—six months pregnant, vaginal bleeding, last child born dead—and I was called into a room mere moments after Steve joined me.

"It must be bad," I said to Steve.

Before I had been in the hospital a half hour, I was wheeled into an ultrasound room. I anxiously watched the screen, looking for my baby's heart.

"There it is," the technician said happily. "Beating strongly. Can you feel all the kicking going on? This baby is active."

Steve grinned. "Told you," he said to me.

"Did you want to know if it's a boy or girl?" the technician asked. "I could easily check for you."

Steve and I looked at each other. We hadn't known in advance for the other kids.

"I want to know," I whispered with renewed excitement.

"Yeah, I do, too." Steve was grinning. "Okay, prove me right again. It's a boy."

"Wrong," he answered a few moments later. "It's a girl. She's definitely a girl."

"A girl! Wow! We're going to have a little girl!" I could hardly believe it.

"Wow. A girl," my husband answered with the same amazed tone.

She had no name yet, but she was ours.

"So then why was I bleeding?" I asked the doctor a little while later, after the heart rate monitor hooked up to my belly continued to indicate the vitality of the child playing inside me.

"It's hard to say. That could have been caused by several factors: mental stress, physical activity, sexual intercourse … among other things. Do any of those sound like possibilities?"

"All three. But it was probably the last thing. Last night was the first time in six months I had sexual intercourse." I didn't want to explain why.

"Ah, well. That explains it." He didn't seem even vaguely interested in the reasoning for my abstinence. "During pregnancy there is increased vasculature in the cervix. The minor trauma of sexual intercourse causes the little blood vessels to break, and vaginal bleeding results."

"So, everything is okay?"

"Everything is okay. However, it's good you came in. When bleeding occurs in a second or third trimester, it's wise to rule out more ominous causes like placenta abruptio or placenta previa."

I nodded. "So, we can go now?" I asked.

"I'm going to ask you to stay for another hour or so to make sure the stress tests remain stable, but then you can go back home and resume normal activity."

"Except sex," Steve said.

"No, even that should be okay. I don't expect to see you folks back in here for about three more months. And that will be to receive your daughter."

We got home at dawn. I went straight to bed and didn't wake up until Simon climbed on me a few hours later.

I held Simon's hand as we worked our way downstairs and then picked up the phone to call Maryann.

"I hope I'm not waking you —" I started.

"What are you talking about?" Maryann interrupted. "I've been waiting by the phone. Is everything okay?"

I looked toward Simon who was crawling toward a pile of magazines. The bright morning sun beat through the windows, and I suddenly saw a glitter between the bookshelf and the wall. I ignored Maryann for a moment and went over to it.

"What is it, Heather?" she said through the receiver.

I laughed. For some reason, I wasn't surprised at what I found: Steve's wedding ring. "Yeah, everything's okay, Maryann. In a few months a beautiful baby girl will join this family."

It was three months to the day.

S teve came home from work and found me curled up on the couch. Even at nine months pregnant, I wasn't often caught snoozing.

"Uh-oh," he said with his eyes on me while welcoming the hugs of his boys. He was smiling.

"Yep," I answered without the smile. "It's starting."

"How far apart are the contractions?"

"Far. Right now I just feel lousy, not agonized. But I think we'll be calling your parents in the morning."

"Come on, let's go run around the block so we can call them sooner," he said with a grin.

"Don't play with me, Steve. I'll kill you with this pillow if I have to. I could easily claim temporary insanity."

"Not self-defense?"

"That too." And then I groaned. "Oh, I hate this."

"Why don't we just call my folks now?" Steve asked.

"Because this might not be the real thing. I don't want to go in with false labor."

"It's the real thing."

"How do you know?"

"Because I've never seen you lounge on the couch with such a sorry expression on your face before. And because you're a day overdue. And because you were dilated to five at yesterday's doctor appointment."

"Okay, but let's still wait a bit."

"It's supposed to go quicker every time, and the other times went pretty quick."

"For you, maybe," I retorted. "I don't want to do this again, Steve."

"You've done this three times already, babe. You can do it again." He gave me a sloppy kiss on the forehead and went to the telephone, whistling. "I'll just tell them to stay near the phone." Each boy clung to one of his legs, and, to their great delight, Steve swung them along as he walked.

I liked Steve's enthusiasm, but I couldn't muster up the strength to join him in it. Instead, I closed my eyes and tried to deny the inevitable.

I made it through the night. Steve woke up every hour or so and asked me if it was time to go. I didn't use my energy to answer. I simply walked from room to room, looking in vain for comfort. At about five in the morning I finally nodded my head to Steve when he asked the question. "Yeah. You'd better call them."

"How far apart are the contractions?"

"Two or three minutes."

"Yikes. Why'd you wait so long to wake me?"

"I wanted to be sure."

Steve called his parents. I called Maryann.

"Don't go over so many bumps," I bellowed to Steve as we sped to the hospital a half hour later.

"I'm not," he said.

I groaned. "I can't even blame this on you this time, can I?"

"You can if it helps." He was grinning at me, but I knew he meant it.

"Why do you always act so happy when I'm in labor?"

"I can't help it. We're going to have a baby today." He was almost giddy.

After another labor pain passed, I looked at Steve and dared to speak my deep longing. "Do you think there is a chance this is your baby?"

"No, not physically." The sun was creeping over the horizon, and Steve's face reflected the melon-colored glow. He looked at me. "But don't even think about that, Heather. We're having a baby. That's all that matters."

"What will the hospital staff think?"

"What do you mean?"

"Here we are, a white couple, and out comes a biracial baby. You'll be all excited, anyway. Will they think you're stupid to not notice or what?"

"Who cares what they think?"

"Well, it will be kind of weird."

"Maybe Maryann will tell them."

I nodded. "Yeah. I should tell her it's okay to tell them. I don't want anyone acting weird when she's born."

"Don't worry about how they'll act. They'll act weird if they know, and they'll act weird if they don't know. Who cares? It's none of their business."

I didn't answer. I was trying to breathe—hooooo-hoo-hoo-hoo—in such a way that my body would relax and could operate at optimal performance. It didn't work. I just hurt. "Never again let me say that giving birth is an amazing experience. I would rather face all the obstacles that confronted Voltaire's Candide than to go through labor and delivery one more time."

"We're almost there," Steve said. "Keep doing that breathing thing."

He tried to drop me off at the emergency entrance we had been at three months ago. "No, I can walk," I said. I suppose the pain was stopping my mind from grasping the truth that procrastination is sometimes impossible.

"Heather, your contractions are just minutes apart. Go in."

"I know. Hurry up and park the dumb car."

Steve had learned by now never to argue with a woman in labor. He parked the car. And he didn't say "I told you so" when he had to practically carry me through the parking lot.

"She's having a baby!" Steve said frantically to the first person he saw when we walked through the doors. "Hurry! She's having a baby!"

I was on a stretcher trying to hoooo-hoo-hoo my way through the pain while the nurse who wheeled us down the hallway chatted happily. "I see that you're Christian Reformed," she said. I was hoping she was going by our paperwork and not our panicked faces. "I am, too," she told us, and then she pointed to a speaker. "Listen to the radio." She laughed softly in the momentary hush. "It was so quiet on the floor tonight, I thought I could get away with putting a Christian station on. Nobody's said a word."

"That's great," Steve said. I suppose there was nothing else to say.

I wiped away a drop of sweat before it slipped into my eye. "Is Dr. DeHaan here yet?" I asked.

"Not yet, sweetie. I'll be taking care of you until you're close to delivery. But don't worry: You'll be getting my full attention. You've pretty much got the floor to yourself."

"Okay. I need to tell you something then." I was able to talk only because I was between contractions. "We've kind of got a unique situation here."

I looked at Steve so he could take over. The nurse looked from me to him.

Steve looked uncomfortable, and I regretted putting him on the spot. My regret passed immediately because another contraction attacked me. When it passed, I continued. "Listen, I need to say this because otherwise I'll be thinking about it when the baby is born, and I don't want anything to taint that moment." I paused only briefly. I had to say it before another contraction struck. "We expect our baby to be biracial. I was raped by a black guy."

"Oh, honey," she started to ooze.

"No," I said quickly. "It's okay. We're excited about having this baby. Just please make sure no one makes a big deal of the baby's race."

She looked like she wanted to stroke me. "I promise you that will be taken care of." We had slowed down and were starting to turn into a room. She stopped and returned me to the hallway with sudden confidence. "No, I'm not putting you in here. You get the VIP room. No one deserves it more than you."

I never thought about the concerns of the staff again.

"You're dilated to 9.5, Heather," Maryann told me moments later. She hadn't waited for the call from the hospital. "What were you trying to do, have the baby in the car?" There was no hint of humor in her voice.

I wanted to cry. "I can't do this again, Maryann."

"Yes, you can," she answered simply as she went about her business calmly. "You're going to do just fine."

Steve laid a blanket over my shivering body. I whipped it off a moment later and moaned. The despair in my voice might have convinced even a bitter enemy to pity me.

"Do you want drugs this time?" Steve asked.

"No. It's almost over anyway, isn't it?" I looked at Maryann imploringly.

Maryann nodded slightly. "I don't think you need an epidural, but I'm definitely going to give you some Demerol. You're shaking uncontrollably." She put a hand on my forehead and smiled softly at me. "Relax, Heather.... Breathe.... You're going to do just fine.... You're strong.... You're going to do just fine."

I hardly noticed the IV the nurse gave me, but my body soon stopped shaking.

Steve held my hand, and I nearly maimed his fingers in response. "I'm cold," I said. But I furiously threw off the blanket he once again gave me. "Maryann," I shouted, "I need to push!"

And then Maryann said what every obstetrician must fear saying to a woman whose labor pains have ripped from her every inhibition, from manners to modesty. A woman gentle in her usual state might turn violent in this one. Maryann said, "Wait."

"Aaahhh!" I wailed. "I need to push!"

Moments—or perhaps years—later I heard my doctor say to her staff, "Alright. I think she's ready. Heather, you may push."

Steve put his mouth to my ear. "Heather, I want you to watch." He pointed to the mirror that the nurse had set up for just that purpose. I hadn't watched any of my other babies being born. "I want you to see this." His words were so soft that I might have ignored them in the midst of my pain, but his uncharacteristic passion caught me. I looked at his face close to mine and saw his moist eyes. "Please."

I pushed, and I saw the crown of my daughter's head. A rush of passion charged through my body. "There she is," I whispered.

The next fifteen minutes of my life were filled with laughter and tears as my husband and I watched the miracle playing out before our eyes: a head, eyes, a mouth, shoulders, and the rest of the tiny perfect, wriggling body.

"She's here," Maryann announced, smiling crazily as she held my baby out to me.

"A girl!" Steve said through tears. "She really is a girl. Heather, we have a baby girl!"

"Rachael Maria Gemmen," I crooned to the child in my arms, exhaustion forgotten. "I'm glad to finally meet you."

CHAPTER FOURTEEN

A
LITTLE
DUTCH
GIRL

If the first Sunday
back in church
after the rape was
emotionally brutal for me,
this first Sunday
back after the birth of our
child was dazzling.

*My fantasies about you bounced between watching your
face on the stand as the judge sentenced you to the chair and
watching your face through a heavy glass as you absorbed the
truth of God's infinite grace. One way or the other, I wanted
your life to be changed radically.*

W hat if he comes back and kidnaps her?" I asked
Steve in our living room the next week. As I stared
down into the face of the little person in my arms, I did not doubt
that a biological parent of Rachael would want her desperately.

"He won't. He's long gone."

Rachael yawned and I smiled. "She's got my sister's nose,
don't you think?" I said.

"I think she looks like you."

"You do?" I was delighted. I searched my daughter's face,
looking for parentage. I saw only beauty in her soft, brown skin
and deep, dark eyes. "I'm glad I didn't see his face. I don't know
if she looks like him or not. I don't want to know."

"Quit talking about him, okay? He's not part of this."

I heard the *vroom-vroom* noises of the boys from the play-room and the cooing of the little girl in my arms. Noises of abundance. I shrugged my shoulders. I didn't mind talking or not talking about the man who had become, in my mind, merely a sperm provider for the most beautiful baby on earth.

"Hand me that blanket, would you?" I said to my husband.

"Are you going to be feeling well enough to go to church tomorrow?" he asked as he tucked the softness around Rachael's little body.

"Are you kidding? I can't wait to show her off. I don't care if I'm half dead."

We were back at Sherman Street. The person who had most influenced Steve and me to return after our two-month sabbatical was a sixty-five-year-old Jamaican man. Financial stress had forced him to leave home more than a decade ago; he missed his family intensely. Every Sunday for several years this grandfather had greeted us with a kiss, pushed candy into the hands of our kids, and reminded us of some good reason to praise God. He had often joined us at our home for a meal after church, bringing with him apples or cider from the farm where he worked. Every Sunday we were gone, he called us at home and told us how tremendous the sermon had been and how much he had missed our presence there. One day he said, in broken English, "Have you call Jon and Barb yet? God not wanting to see the body broken. Yous need to figure things out and then come worship the Lord together."

We wrote a letter to Jon and Barb, apologizing for hurting them and asking them to please forgive us. We didn't get a response, but we went back to our church family.

If the first Sunday back in church after the rape was emotionally brutal for me, this first Sunday back after the birth of our child was dazzling. We showed up early because I had anticipated some enthusiasm over our newborn, but there was no way I could have prepared myself for the passionate expressions of welcome that bombarded this youngest and most famous member of the congregation.

"My granddaughter," said our Jamaican friend with tears in his eyes. He has called her by no other name since.

"A little Heather," said another friend, one who had often enjoyed late-night conversations at our house and so knew what he was talking about. "Look out, world!"

"She is a miracle," said an older, Dutch gentleman whose frequent words of encouragement had often nurtured my soul. He took Rachael from my arms and paraded her through the church, beaming as joyously as would a young boy with a remote-controlled airplane.

Amidst all the gushing over my baby's soft curls and tiny newness, I heard a word of hope: "Heather," said a middle-aged woman whose husband a few years previously had fallen from a ladder to his death. Her compassion for others had not been diminished by her loss. "I know of some kids who need a home. Do you think the Adamses would be interested in adopting a sibling group?" Two girls and a boy, ages one, two, and three. Available immediately.

"It's sure worth asking them," I said with enthusiasm.

"I didn't even know they were looking to adopt," she said. "Gosh, there are so many kids needing a home, I'm sure something will work out for them."

"I hope so. Please do call them. I know it would mean a lot to them."

The music in the sanctuary increased in volume, and the stragglers sneaked in. I stayed in the quiet foyer to nurse Rachael and then joined Steve and the boys.

My Dutch friend preached that Sunday with an accent that

made me nostalgic for home. He read the story about Jacob wrestling with an angel. "Don't go unless you bless me," Jacob had said to the angel after an all-night struggle. "Don't let your pain be for nothing," my friend interpreted. "Ask God to bless you in your struggles, to let you grow from them." I felt conspicuous, like this sermon was preached specifically to me—until I looked around and saw the people who surrounded me: men and women strong by the grace of God through their trials.

H ow are you feeling, Heather?" asked one of my girl-friends after church. "Are you still up for dinner at my in-laws'?"

Steve had thought the invitation odd at first. "Why would we want to hang out at their parents' house? We don't even know them."

But I loved the idea of getting to know our friends on another level. We would get to see the house our friend grew up in and meet the people who raised him. "Besides," I said, "I hear that Mrs. Vaandering cooks a mean dinner. I bet it'll be as good as my oma's Christmas dinner."

It was. We crowded around a cozy dining room table with placemats and cloth napkins and lovely china, eating mashed potatoes with thick brown gravy, buttery green beans, and tender roast beef cooked to perfection.

"A preacher with a Dutch accent and then a meal like only the Dutch can make," I said appreciatively.

"Ah, *schatje*," Mrs. Vaandering said, "you are Dutch, then, too?"

"My parents are both immigrants." I knew it would impress them. I intended to inspire them with my knowledge of all things Dutch, but Rachael woke up and demanded to be fed. I retired into the living room where the couch and straight-backed chairs had doilies over the armrests. I looked around at the family pictures hanging on the walls and at the knickknacks on the dusted piano as I listened to the humorous stories Mr. Vaandering told about his son. I made it back to the table just as dessert was being passed around.

"Let me burp her while you enjoy a little something, eh?" Mrs. Vaandering said, taking Rachael from my arms. I happily complied and dove into my warm apple crisp topped with a generous amount of ice cream. "Less than a week old, eh?" she said, crooning at our baby. "Beautiful. But I see she has some jaundice."

Rachael had no jaundice. I didn't say anything.

"Yes, you'll want to keep an eye on that. Her skin is so dark," Mrs. Vaandering said, gently touching Rachael's perfect cheek.

"Mmm-hmmm," I murmured. I glanced at our friend. He cringed. I could see he hadn't told her.

"I mean, she just doesn't look like a little Dutch girl, does she?" Mrs. Vaandering looked up at me. I saw her eyes move over to Steve and then fall back on the face of the baby she held. "No, not a little Dutch girl at all." She looked up at the boys who had devoured their food, and I saw her watching their faces as she offered the backyard to them. They ran out happily.

I wondered for a moment if I should tell her why the daughter of my womb didn't look the same as her brothers. But I quickly dismissed the idea. It wasn't exactly dinner-table talk, and I hated the idea of her thinking of me always as "that girl who was raped." Secretly, I was pleased my friends hadn't considered the point worth telling their parents. I was simply their friend, not "that girl."

I got a phone call from Mrs. Vaandering that evening. "Oh, my dear," she said, "I am mortified over my blunder of this afternoon. Please, please forgive me if I embarrassed you."

I laughed, genuinely amused by the memory of the confusion. "I was embarrassed, but you don't need to apologize.

You had no idea. I guess I'm going to have to prepare myself for those kinds of situations. No one is going to walk around in front of me all my life, cueing people in to what they should say to me."

I didn't know how true my words were.

In the diaper section of the grocery store a woman gushed over Rachael and asked me which country she was from. "From here," I answered stupidly.

"Wow. Good for you. We had to go with foreign adoption because we were tired of waiting so long. What agency did you use?"

I wanted to turn around and walk away. What could I say? Should I say she's not adopted and open myself up for further questions … or silent suspicions? Should I let this stranger continue to believe my baby was adopted and so lie in front of my kids … and rob myself of hard-earned motherhood?

"Listen," I said, "I'd love to talk, but I'm kind of in a rush."

Our family was eating pizza at a restaurant near our home when Rachael was just a month old. Deshawn was with us. "Wow!" said the waitress. "Are these all your kids?" I didn't blame her for asking: We were an eclectic group. But I still cringed.

"It's a long story," I told her and then ordered our meal.

I nursed Rachael in the club nursery before taking off for a game of racquetball with Steve. "Don't ask!" my aura screamed, in vain, to the older woman who hovered in to ask, in a hushed voice, if my *husband* would be picking her up or not. "He is your husband, isn't he?" she whispered conspiratorially.

Rachael was sleeping in the stroller by the time I reached the playground with the boys, and her sweet face attracted the attention of some of the moms who were there. "What a doll," a thirty-something black woman said to me. "Are you watching her for someone?"

"No," I said, reaching down to adjust the visor over my

daughter. "She's mine." Inwardly, I wondered why I had to answer all these questions to every stranger I met. Outwardly, I smiled graciously.

"Sister," the woman answered, "what you got one of our babies for?" She laughed and touched my arm kindly. I laughed, too. I didn't know what else to do.

"That's obvious, ain't it?" another mom answered. "She got one of our men." Before I could respond—more accurately, before I could think of a response—she said, "And them boys are yours, too?"

"Not the oldest," I said in reference to Deshawn. "He's our neighbor."

"Mmmm-hmmm," the second woman said, laughing, she thought, knowingly.

I wanted Tasha around to protect me.

"That's alright, sister," the first woman said to me. "I don't blame you for wanting some black magic."

I suppose I should have just told some of these people the truth. Maybe "I was raped" would have given them reason to pause in the future before they blurted out their thoughts and questions. But so many people knew already. Having every acquaintance know my most personal story was hard enough; telling every stranger I met was beyond my strength.

The one person who had the right to question Rachael's presence, didn't. "Let me take her," Steve said one night after I had finished a midnight feeding. "You need some sleep."

I woke up a few hours later to find Steve making baby faces to the little girl who wouldn't sleep. I nearly wept at the sight of their bonding. "Steve, thank you so much for being such a good dad to her," I said with conviction.

Steve waved away my praise. "She's my girl. What else would I do? Now get out of here before she starts crying for you."

I went back to sleep and didn't wake up until I heard the doorbell ring. It woke the boys, too. Chad, Simon, and I went downstairs to find Deshawn's nose pressed against the glass and Rachael's nose deep in Steve's neck. She, like her dad, was sound asleep.

"Come on in," I whispered to Deshawn. "But we all have to be really quiet." I pointed to the sleeping couple on the couch. Deshawn giggled.

Dolores stopped by later that day. "The damn landlord just kicked me out," she told me by the door. "Can Deshawn spend the night with you?"

"Of course he can," I answered promptly. "How about you? We've got plenty of room."

"Nah. I'll be alright."

Dolores came by the next day. "I ain't got a place, yet. Can he stay with you awhile longer?"

I told her it was okay, so she walked to the street and reached into the trunk of her friend's Monte Carlo and pulled out a garbage bag.

"Here's his stuff," she said, dropping it heavily on my front step. Her friend honked the horn from behind tinted windows, and Dolores left without talking to her son. I waved good-bye and then approached the bag warily. It smelled like something I took home from a weeklong camping trip.

A few days passed, and no one talked about how long Deshawn would be staying. On the fourth day, while I was transplanting Snow-on-the-Mountain from beside my garage to the front yard under a maple tree, I saw Dolores walking toward the house on the other side of the street. She drew closer but didn't cross over. I stopped what I was doing to greet her, but she only waved and walked on.

Deshawn didn't seem to wonder about his future. He was having a blast with us—going swimming at the Y, visiting the zoo, hanging out at the beach. He slept soundly at night and never asked about his mom, so I didn't worry about him.

A week later, Dolores showed up at our door. "I still don't have a place, but I'm going to buy him something. Where is he?"

"He's in the backyard. I'll show you."

Dolores and Deshawn walked to a convenience store around the corner. Deshawn came home with a huge smile and a bag of beef jerky. Dolores was gone before I could see her again.

"She makes me so mad," I told Steve after dinner while the kids were out playing. "I don't mind that Deshawn is here, but she should give us an idea of how long he's staying. And she should come visit him more often."

"I have a feeling he'll be staying a long time."

"Yeah, it may take her awhile to find a place. What if she never does?"

"Like I said, he'll be staying here a long time."

I looked at my husband and smiled. I leaned over to kiss him. "You're amazing," I said.

"What?"

"I always complain that you never show your love, but really, you love deeper than most people do. It seems like everyone else's love is based on feelings; yours is based on action."

"Whatever you say," Steve said. A few minutes later he went out to the garage to work on the bookshelf he was building me.

"I was tucking the kids in bed that night when Deshawn dropped the bomb. "I'm going to live in Guatemala."

"Guatemala? Why?"

"My mom has some friends there who will take care of me."

"Well, why go all the way to Guatemala to find someone who will take care of you? You can stay with us."

I saw Deshawn's eyes move slowly up to look into mine. He seemed to be holding his breath. "Forever?" he said quietly.

Only two other promises in my life met the depth of the

words I spoke to that young boy: One promise was to God, the other to my husband.

"Deshawn," I said, pulling him close, "if it's what you and your mom want, you may stay with us forever."

Deshawn remained silent for a long moment, his head down. Finally he looked up at me again. "Why can't my mom take care of me?"

I knew so little of Dolores's life. I had no idea how deep her pain was. But at that moment I didn't care. I wanted to shake her. I wanted to scream, "Quit being so selfish! Give up your crack and your boyfriends so that you can be a mother to your child! We all have lousy stuff in our lives. But we deal with it! You don't have the luxury of living in despair, okay? You have a son who needs you!"

But Dolores wasn't around to hear my admonition. She had chosen a different path.

"Listen, babe," I said softly. "Your mom loves you a lot. But she needs to take care of herself before she can take care of you. I promise you that I will pray for her, and I know that God cares deeply about her. As soon as she discovers God's love for her, she will be able to take care of you again, okay?"

"Okay," he said. "I'll pray, too."

A few weeks later, Dolores came to our doorstep again. "I can't come in," she said. "I'm in a rush. I just want to make sure my boy is okay."

"He's doing very well," I told her. "But he misses you."

"I know. But I don't have a place yet."

"He can stay here as long as you like, Dolores. We love having him. But if you think it's going to be much longer, we should probably make this legal. I've been signing his school papers and stuff."

"What do you mean, legal?" she asked defensively.

"I think it would be good if Steve and I could be Deshawn's

guardians. As soon as you get settled, guardianship will go back to you. I'm just afraid we're going to get into trouble if I keep signing his stuff."

"Will it cost anything?"

"No," I lied. I knew we would be covering the costs. "All you have to do is sign some papers. I've got them already. Do you have a few minutes to look them over?"

Dolores didn't read the papers, but she signed them.

"Do you have a number I can reach you at so I can tell you the court date?" I asked.

"Court? I ain't going to no court."

"You don't have to if you don't want to. No show means you agree with the proceedings."

Dolores's eyes narrowed. "You better not be screwing me," she said, wagging a finger in my face.

My manners stepped aside so I could lean toward her. "I'm taking care of your son, Dolores," I said softly, threateningly. "If you don't trust me, you shouldn't be leaving him here."

Dolores backed away. "Nah," she said. "I trust you."

I stepped toward her. "What I want more than anything is to see you settled down so that Deshawn can have his mother back."

"I will, I will." She turned to leave. "I'm working on something right now." From the sidewalk she called out a thank-you and then disappeared down the street.

I looked at Deshawn carefully that day when he came home from school. He was energetically telling me about the back flip he did off the teeter-totter and how all the kids wanted him to do it again and how his teacher said he should take gymnastics and not do things like that at school. As I stared into the face of the little person before me, I wondered how his biological parent could not want him desperately.

And I knew Rachael was safe.

CHAPTER FIFTEEN

MOUNTAIN MOVEMENT

I had been beyond hope before, and that had never stopped God.

Did you grow up on these streets? Is the steady beat of rap music your chant of meditation? Are the street corners your sanctuary? Or is this a place that taught you despair, a place from which you long to escape? For me the city was neither home nor prison: It was a path.

W ould you ever move to Colorado, Steve?" I asked doubtfully after the dinner dishes had been cleared away. It was a humid August afternoon, and the sidewalks seemed to steam under the men and women who were taking lazy walks, waving to each other and smelling the food grilling in backyards. We didn't have air conditioning, so our windows were wide open. I could hear Rachael's four-year-old laughter drifting over the voices of her three big brothers as they ran through the sprinkler in the yard.

"I'd move tomorrow," Steve answered promptly.

"Yeah, right."

"I would," he insisted, glancing up from his book.

"You'd better think carefully about what you're saying. I got a job offer today."

I was working at a large Christian publishing house as an editor of children's books. A former colleague had called me up that day to say that she needed to hire an editor, and she needed to know right away if I would come.

"Are you serious?" Steve asked. "Move to Colorado?"

"Yeah. Colorado Springs. We'd have to go next month."

"Let's get packing."

"Be serious."

"I am. Are you?"

"Well, the job sounds ideal, but it's pretty far away."

"Wow." He got up to get a map. He spread it out on the dining room table. "Colorado Springs! We could take daytrips into the mountains to go skiing. We could go hiking on a mountain trail on a Sunday afternoon. Colorado is gorgeous."

"As long as there would be no humidity." A fan was blowing on us, but my hot skin still felt sticky.

"No humidity. No mosquitoes."

"And no family," I said. "No friends." I dropped into a chair.

"The kids are getting big now," he said. "It's not like they wouldn't know our families. And we'd come back to visit."

"Remember when we were first married how mad I would get when your mom brought us groceries every time she came over? Now I don't know what we'd do without your family."

"She hardly ever does that anymore. We'd be fine without them."

"I'm not talking about the food. I'm talking about them. And we'd be moving farther away from my family, too. What if we got lonely?"

"We'll make friends. You'll probably be having people over every night of the week before we've been there even a month."

"I don't know. I can't imagine finding friends like we have

now. Think of them: Maryann and Byron. Tasha. Jon and Barb. Everyone at church. We've been through a lot together. I don't think we'll ever find friendships like that again."

"It doesn't seem likely. But remember when it didn't seem likely we would ever be friends with Jon and Barb again? Or with Tasha? And that all worked out."

I am still in wonder that it all worked out. Our friendship with the Adamses was restored when the four of us were able to see past our own despair enough to care for each other's wounds. For Jon and Barb, this happened when they adopted the sibling group a woman at our church had introduced them to. Jon and Barb found their hearts' desire fulfilled with not just one but with three children they called their own.

My relationship with Tasha didn't heal so quickly. At church we avoided each other—me, because I was afraid of saying anything inappropriate; her, because I already had. When she moved to another city, we lost touch altogether. A few years later, I heard her voice on the other end of the telephone line asking if we could please renew our relationship, and I felt like she had handed me a glass slipper: I was startled and delighted by the gift that fit me so naturally.

"Yes, it all worked out," I answered Steve, "but only because God orchestrated it—"

"So you don't think God can orchestrate things again?"

"Well ..." I didn't have an answer to that.

"Besides, we would still be friends with them."

"Okay. But what about living in the city? Are we supposed to give that up?"

Steve was silent for a moment before he answered. I didn't interrupt his thoughts. "I think it's alright if we leave," he said. "We've fulfilled our purpose here."

I nodded my head. Steve's wisdom had grown over the years

so that I now looked to him for spiritual direction. "Okay, maybe God is calling us to something else," I agreed. "But I like it here. Why did he want us here when we didn't like it, and now that we do, we're not called to it anymore?"

"I don't know. I don't think we'll ever really get the method behind God's madness. I just know that we've got a chance to move to the Rockies." He pointed to Colorado Springs on the map and then looked sideways at me. "Pike's Peak is right here, Heather. And the Garden of the Gods. Instead of gushing over fall colors for a few weeks of the year, you'll be looking at a snow-peaked mountain every day."

It did sound like a dream come true. And the job seemed perfectly designed for me. I let go of my fear and jumped whole-heartedly into the adventure.

"Okay," I said, standing up. "Let's do it."

"Seriously?"

"Yes. I'm going to go call right now." I was halfway to the phone.

"Wait. We should think about it some more. What about work for me? I'll have to look for a job," he said.

"You'll find something. Construction is booming there. Or maybe I'll make enough money so you can stay home with the kids."

"That sounds good," he said longingly. "But—"

"Come on, Steve. Let's go for it. Let's step out of all that's familiar to us and see what happens. It'll be fun. It'll be good for us."

"But next month already?" Steve asked apprehensively.

Rachael ran into the house at that moment, dripping water behind her. Her laughter revealed delighted fear; Simon was chasing her with a water gun. She stopped long enough to kiss me and hug Steve, and then she tore out of the house again with Simon right behind her.

"Why wait?" I asked my husband. "Don't you want to see what's going to happen next?"

What happened next was a blur of action. We quit our jobs and started packing. We visited friends and family, crying our good-byes. We sold our house and secured new housing. And then we drove across the country to our new home.

Deshawn came with us. I had contacted his mom to let her know we were moving. "You know I want him back," Dolores told me. "As soon as I get me a place, he's coming back to live with me."

"Okay," I said. I didn't remind her that she had been saying that for three years. "But you're okay with our taking him to Colorado with us?"

"I guess so," she responded.

It wasn't so easy for Deshawn. A darkness of heart seeped into this young child whose outlook on life, as long as I had known him, had been joyful and compassionate. Now, he lashed out in anger at everyone. "I want to go back to Michigan," he spat. "I want to go back to my real mom."

"I think you should tell her that," I told him. I was beyond hoping for reconciliation for them—in the last three years she had rejected him more times than I, let alone he, could bear. But I had been beyond hope before, and that had never stopped God. "Maybe if she knows how much you want her, she'll be motivated to find a place," I offered.

I loved Deshawn as deeply as I loved each of the other kids God had picked out for me—and I didn't want to see him go; but I knew Dolores, even with all her faults, was the one Deshawn was looking to for acceptance.

"She *will* take me back!" Deshawn shouted with accusation in his voice. "You don't think she will, but she will!"

I nodded. "It's important that you try to reunite with your mother. And as much as it hurts me to see you go, I will do what I can to help you." His customary embraces were noticeably absent. "But, Deshawn—" I began. I didn't finish the sentence until he finally looked begrudgingly up at me. "If your mom is not able to take you back, could we please adopt you?"

He walked to the phone without looking at me.

To my surprise, Dolores promised her son the world. "Yes, baby," she gushed. "I've got everything worked out. In two months, at the most, I'll have a place for us. I've already talked to the landlord. And I just started a real good job yesterday. Oh, baby! I can't wait for us to be together again."

We both believed her—he with great joy; I with gladness, fear, and sorrow.

At his request, we returned Deshawn to Michigan right away so he could get back into the Christian school he had been attending. He stayed with a family from Sherman Street. "Just for a few months," we told them. "He's going back to his mom."

But two months turned to four. Four turned to six. I talked to Dolores more during those months than I had all the years we were neighbors. Coaching her. Cajoling her. Begging her. I wanted Deshawn back with us, but I couldn't bear to see him rejected by his mom again.

I suppose I shouldn't have believed her promises, but I couldn't help it that she failed again.

The school year ended, and Deshawn came home to us. The first thing he said after he welcomed my hug was, "Mom, will you and Dad adopt me now?"

We did, and at that moment, my heart could not contain any more joy.

Every time I look at the mountains, it is a new experience. Whether Pike's Peak is mirroring the sunrise so the entire horizon, east and west, is lit with a multi-colored glow; whether its silhouette is etched for miles onto a darkening sky; whether black thunderclouds are hurling rain onto the Front Range, emphasizing its unchanging strength; whether the brilliant snow is harshly reflecting a late-afternoon winter sun; whether the hills look green and hazy and deceptively gentle—the experience is good.

Mountains reveal vastness, drawing from me an awareness, not of insignificance, but still of smallness. It is the *moods* of the mountains, however, that propel me into reflection—variance displayed on the unmoving; fleetingness passing over the ageless—and I dare to walk forward on unknown paths.

STARTLING
BEAUTY

Rape takes too much.
But I, for one,
have gained more than
I have lost.

Rape is ugliness at its basest form. Rape destroys innocence and cultivates bitterness. It steals security and extends fear. It kills hope and fosters shame.

Rape leaves no room for beauty.

"My father raped me when I was eighteen," a woman told me in the privacy of her living room. She was the mother of two young children, the wife of a godly man. "I hadn't seen him in ten years, but he came here yesterday and tried to rape me again." Her voice wobbled as she tried to say words that resisted articulation.

My face grew wet as I sat with her in the silence.

"I hate him, Heather," she whispered. "I'll always hate him."

I don't know why I believed him," a twenty-year-old sobbed. "He broke into my apartment, and I still trusted him."

"What happened?"

"I pushed the dresser up against my bedroom door so he

couldn't get in. He stood outside the door for an hour, trying to convince me that he would protect me if I would only open the door. I finally did, and then he raped me."

She curled up on the couch, clutching her knees to her chest.

I put a blanket over her. "He caused your terror and then used it for his advantage," I told her. "It wasn't your fault."

"I'm so scared," she whispered into the air. "If I'm that easy to trick, how can I face life again?"

W ho needs men?" quipped a middle-aged woman who had been raped on the first date she attempted after her divorce.

She dropped out of counseling and took up drinking. She left the church and joined a feminist group.

"Not all men are bad," I ventured.

"Ha! You should know better than that!"

"I do know. I know many men who are not like the men who raped us."

"Oh, Heather, don't be so naïve. If they smile now, they'll bite you later."

R ape takes too much.
  But I, for one, have gained more than I have lost. I have been startled by beauty in places it doesn't belong. I see it on a bloodied cross, and bitterness loses its power. I see it on the face of the man who keeps his vows to me, and fear releases its grip. I see it in the graceful dance of a child who was so unwanted, and hope revives its song.

I consider that our present sufferings are not worth comparing with the glory that will be revealed....

I am convinced that neither death nor life, neither angels nor demons, neither the present nor the future, nor any powers, neither height nor depth, nor anything else in all creation, will be able to separate us from the love of God that is in Christ Jesus our Lord.

from Romans 8

STARTLING
BEAUTY

Study Guide
for Personal Reflection
and Group Discussion

B eauty is startling when it appears in the face of stark ugliness. The tiny fingers of a stillborn baby. Trusting relationships in a dangerous neighborhood. A cherished child conceived through rape.

Startling Beauty narrates Heather's journey between despair and hope as she faces pain no one should experience. Relationships are strained and mended; decisions are forced and welcomed; fears are created and calmed; faith is threatened and increased. Heather and her husband, Steve, fall into grace, exchanging their emptiness for God's fullness.

We can't help but marvel at the beauty of this exchange, just as we would ooh and ahh over a beautiful display of fireworks. But the individual bursts of glory don't compare to the beauty of the grand finale, when we see this exchange happening in the lives of God's children.

And God is just waiting to lavish his startling grace on you.

After reading Heather's story and vicariously experiencing the depth of her despair, you may find yourself face to face with your own. Old wounds may be opened, and you don't know where turn. God created a longing within you to step into the restoration he offers through Jesus Christ, but you may not know exactly how to take this step.

Answering the questions provided, privately or with a group, will strengthen you for the journey into restoration. Ask the Holy Spirit to direct you, refer to the Bible passages recommended at the end of the guide, and spend plenty of time in prayer.

It takes incredible courage to pursue healing, but God will not leave you to face this task alone. Romans 5:17 says that "God's abundant provision of grace" restores us. Abundant. The extent of God's fullness from which he provides for us is limitless.

"And my God will meet all your needs
according to his glorious riches in Christ Jesus."
–Philippians 4:19

Chapter One
STATIC IN THE STORM

1. "I've always believed that we each choose our own path, but … I … realized for the first time that we don't get to choose the obstacles we face on the journey." Lying on the obstetrician's table, wondering if her baby is still alive, Heather prays, "Oh, God, don't let this be my obstacle. Let me learn about life another way." Do you ever wish you could "trade in" your circumstances? Give an example of how you or someone you know has changed for the better because of a painful life experience.

2. An age-old question that nearly every person confronts in life is this: Why do bad things happen to good people? What experience has forced you to wrestle with this question? How have you resolved it?

3. In this chapter, Heather admits that she often used humor as a "shield," hoping that laughter might keep away the sorrow. What are some other ways people try to protect themselves from the pain of difficult circumstances? Winston Churchill once said, "When you're going through hell, keep going." When is it beneficial to retreat from pain and when is it beneficial to work through it?

Chapter Two
HEAVY EMPTINESS

1. "Self-pity smothered the joy I longed to have." What motivated Heather to let go of her self-pity? When you indulge in self-pity, what does it take to free you from it?

2. Racism is another issue addressed in this book. For a little while, Heather viewed her inner-city neighborhood romantically, but not for long. She says, "I'm not sure when my attitude changed … maybe I was watching the world instead of heaven." Have you ever known that you were departing from the will of God and suffered the consequences for it? What brought you back?

3. "I didn't enjoy my resentment—I hated it—but I didn't know how to change my heart." If we are unable to change ourselves, how will change occur? What are the advantages and disadvantages of allowing God to change your heart?

Chapter Three
PAINFUL HEALING

1. "Strange. Why have I always thought reconciliation was something sweet and gentle?" What is your definition of reconciliation? Racial issues are not the only arena where reconciliation needs to take place. Are there relationships in your family or community that need to be restored? How can you move toward reconciliation?

2. As Heather delves deeper into her racist views, she realizes her own part in the problem. She prays, "Something needs to change, God. Is it me? Again?" Sometimes it's hard to admit that we could be a big part of our own problems. What role have you played in your own difficult circumstances?

3. Heather's circumstances did not change, but her attitude did. How did Heather's change of heart affect her and those around

her? Why do we hang on to beliefs and behaviors that hurt us, when we know letting go will improve our lives?

Chapter Four
THE PAINTING

1. As Heather describes the terrifying details of the rape, she speaks directly to the man who raped her. Why do you think Heather chose this method of relating her story? What would you like to say to the person who most hurt you?

2. "Perhaps the agony [of the rape] would have been too much for me if I hadn't discovered a Place in myself where the Comforter dwelt.... I entered the Place ... and leaned into Holy arms." What do you think Heather meant by a "Place where the Comforter dwelt"? Have you found that place in your own heart where the Comforter dwells?

3. "'Forgive him, Lord.' The words were not even my own." What was your reaction when you read these words?

4. The title of this chapter is "The Painting." Heather speaks of God's brushstrokes upon the canvas of life. What is taking shape on the canvas of your life?

Chapter Five
VIOLATED AGAIN

1. In the aftermath of the rape, Heather finds herself gripped by fear. Fear is a powerful tormentor. What fears have you overcome, and how?

2. "It was my fault." Even in the midst of her trauma, Heather accused herself of negligence. What did you think when you found out she hadn't locked the door?

3. "What are you folks doing in this neighborhood, anyway?" Do you think Heather and Steve chose poorly by staying in the city? Why or why not?

Chapter Six
ILLUSIONS LOST

1. Heather's strengths, as she lists them, include independence, tenacity, and trust. Was she compromising these strengths by leaning on her husband during this stressful time? Why is it sometimes hard to accept comfort and strength from others?

2. One of Heather's core beliefs is the sanctity of life. Name some of your core beliefs and explain why they are important to you. Have you ever had a core belief challenged? If so, how did you respond?

3. "Integrity is so much more than claiming noble ethics.... Integrity is living out expressed beliefs. It is making choices that accurately reflect core values." Do you agree with Heather's assessment of integrity? Why or why not?

4. "Etiquette placed me on the bull's-eye of Fear's assault." Why do we allow manners to have so much power over us? How do we balance caring for others with caring for self?

Chapter Seven
KNOWING BETTER

1. "Mark and Lori's love knocked me into grace. I would have fallen sooner had I known how soft the landing would be." Has anyone ever given you the gift of true compassion? How is human compassion a picture of God's grace?

2. As Heather's friends rally around her, she takes comfort in their concern. She gains strength from their prayers. Do you think our prayers for each other really make a difference? Why or why not?

3. The three most influential people in Heather's life all counseled her to take the pill. She did, despite inner misgivings. When making a decision, how much weight do you give to the advice of others?

Chapter Eight
WALKING ON WATER

1. "You just looking for an easy way out of forgiving him," Tasha told Heather. "If it weren't so bad, then you don't need to forgive much. He done you wrong, sister. And you need to forgive the whole awful thing." What are some barriers to forgiveness? Tell about a time in your life when you chose to forgive.

2. "The idea of healing more quickly [by talking about the rape] seemed remote, or perhaps unrealistic." Why do we sometimes resist talking things out when we know we can't heal on our own? On the other hand, sometimes we wallow in our pain,

talking rather than actively pursuing healing. How would you advise a hurting person who seems stuck?

3. Heather describes the tangible outpouring of love she received—meals, money, babysitting. How do you help someone when the situation she is facing makes you uncomfortable?

Chapter Nine
DOOR NUMBER FOUR

1. After the rape, Heather realizes that she has lost her "innocent faith"—faith that God would use her to bring healing to the inner city. "It didn't seem so easy anymore," she says. How have you dealt with disillusionment or loss of faith in your own life?

2. Steve suggests that Heather get an abortion, and, in her desperation, she consents to the idea. If she had gone through with it, what problems would have been solved? What problems would have been created?

3. How did God intervene in Heather's life? How has he intervened in yours?

Chapter Ten
COMPROMISE

1. Heather and Steve's pastor, Mark, plays a key role in helping them through the healing process. What qualities in Mark made his counsel trustworthy? How can we cultivate these qualities in ourselves?

2. *Startling Beauty* gives numerous examples of people who have suffered. Describe different responses to pain—whether in this book or in your own experience—and discuss which responses bring the most satisfaction, for the short-term and the long-term.

3. As Heather and Steve work through this situation, they discuss the possibility of adoption. If they had gone through with it, what problems would have been solved? What problems would have been created?

Chapter Eleven
CONNECTION

1. "I ... discovered ... how deep love goes when tragedy binds you together," Heather says. In what way has tragedy connected you to another person, and in what way has it separated you from another person? How has tragedy connected or separated you from God?

2. Heather's two best friends did not always tell her what she wanted to hear, but they usually told her what she needed to hear. When is it worth the risk of alienating others by speaking the truth? How do we earn the right to confront?

3. Heather compares a healthy church to a small town: "There are no secrets." Did you consider Heather's closeness to the Sherman Street community to be an advantage or a disadvantage to her? Would you want to be part of such a community? Why or why not?

Chapter Twelve
DESTINY

1. "God, I'm off death row, but I'm not yet free. Please, please make me better." In the past year, how have you grown spiritually, emotionally, relationally, and intellectually? What things do you still need to change in your life?

2. Steve expresses some honest doubts about God. He says, "It's a joke when people pray for God to intervene.... He just doesn't bother himself with that stuff. God made the world self-sufficient, and then he sat back and let us take care of ourselves." Do you agree with this view? Why or why not?

3. Heather is saddened when Tasha ends their friendship, and she realizes that perhaps she has taken Tasha for granted. What do you think Heather's next step should be? What happens when two people are reunited without experiencing reconciliation?

Chapter Thirteen
BABY

1. "Faith is a journey, but there are definite moments along the way when truth propels a person from one state of being to another. I can name several defining moments in my life." For Heather, one of those moments was when her daughter was born. Can you point to a specific moment when your life was changed by truth?

2. "For some reason, I wasn't surprised at what I found: Steve's wedding ring." Do you think Heather and Steve's marriage

improved? If so, how? Have you found that relationships are worth working for?

3. "The next fifteen minutes of my life were filled with laughter and tears as my husband and I watched the miracle playing out before our eyes.... 'A girl!' Steve said through tears." What was the miracle?

Chapter Fourteen
A LITTLE DUTCH GIRL

1. "Don't let your pain be for nothing.... Ask God to bless you in your struggles, to let you grow from them." Can you see that your spiritual or personal growth was affected differently depending on how you responded to painful experiences? Please explain.

2. "Steve, thank you so much for being such a good dad to her," Heather tells her husband. Steve's answer reveals his changed heart: "She's my girl. What else would I do?" Steve moved from wanting to abort the child to embracing her as his own. Have you ever had a radical change of heart despite unchanging circumstances? Talk about it.

3. Heather didn't want everyone to think of her as "that girl who was raped." How can we support others without undermining their dignity?

4. Steve and Heather put their love into action by taking their neighbor boy, Deshawn, into their home. Sometimes God calls us to love one another in ways that are not easy or convenient.

Has anyone ever shown selfless love to you? How is your life different because of this person's love?

Chapter Fifteen
MOUNTAIN MOVEMENT

1. Tasha contacted Heather, asking to renew their friendship. Heather says, "I felt like [Tasha] had handed me a glass slipper: I was startled and delighted by the gift that fit me so naturally." Is someone in your life waiting for you to take the first step toward reconciliation? What would it require for you to take that step?

2. Heather chose to tell others about her traumatic experience. Even though there were times she regretted that choice, she healed more quickly because of it. What are some good reasons for sharing our struggles with others? Are there good reasons for choosing not to share our pain with others?

Epilogue
STARTLING BEAUTY

In the epilogue of *Startling Beauty*, we see that God has brought Heather full circle. She is now ministering to others who have been deeply wounded. No matter how you have been wounded, God loves you unconditionally. How would your life change if this love took root in your heart?

The following scripture passages will enhance your study and discussion.

Chapter One: Static in the Storm
1. Gen. 37–45   2. Heb. 12:7–13   3. Phil. 1:6

Chapter Two: Heavy Emptiness
1. John 13:34–35   2. Ps. 119:105–106   3. Ps. 51

Chapter Three: Painful Healing
1. 2 Cor. 5:11–21   2. Matt. 7:1–5   3. Gal. 5:22–26

Chapter Four: The Painting
1. Eph. 4:14–16   2. Jer. 8:18   3. Luke 23:34
4. Phil. 4:4–9

Chapter Five: Violated Again
1. Gen. 4:7   2. Isa. 50:8   3. Gen. 6–8

Chapter Six: Illusions Lost
1. Eph. 5:22–33   2. 1 Peter 3:15–16   3. Titus 2
4. Matt. 10:12–16

Chapter Seven: Knowing Better
1. Rom. 3:21–31   2. Rom. 8:26–27   3. Job

Chapter Eight: Walking on Water
1. Matt. 18:21–35   2. Ps. 109:21–31   3. Jas. 2:14–17

Chapter Nine: Door Number Four
1. Heb. 11   2. Isa. 30:1–5   3. Matt. 10:29–31

Chapter Ten: Compromise
1. 2 Chron. 1:7–17   2. 2 Cor. 4:6–12

Chapter Eleven: Connection
1. Rom. 8:28–39   3. Heb. 10:24–25

Chapter Twelve: Destiny
1. 1 Peter 2:1–3   2. Matt. 21:18–22   3. Matt. 5:23–24

Chapter Thirteen: Baby
1. Isa. 6:1–8   2. Gen. 2:20–25   3. Rom. 8:28

Chapter Fourteen: A Little Dutch Girl
1. Gen. 32:22–32   2. 1 Thess. 5:16–18   3. Heb. 12:1–3

Chapter Fifteen: Mountain Movement
1. Hosea   2. Ps. 78:1–5

Epilogue
Ps. 37

STARTLING COURAGE

Helping a Friend
Move Beyond Rape to Restoration

HEATHER GEMMEN
AND
IRENE OUDYK-SUK, MACS, MSW

STARTLING JOY

A 90-day Journey out of Despair

HEATHER GEMMEN

The Word at Work Around the World

What would you do if you wanted to share God's love with children on the streets of your city? That's the dilemma David C. Cook faced in 1870's Chicago. His answer was to create literature that would capture children's hearts.

Out of those humble beginnings grew a worldwide ministry that has used literature to proclaim God's love and disciple generation after generation. Cook Communications Ministries is committed to personal discipleship—to helping people of all ages learn God's Word, embrace his salvation, walk in his ways, and minister in his name.

Faith Kidz, RiverOak, Honor, Life Journey, Victor, NextGen . . . every time you purchase a book produced by Cook Communications Ministries, you not only meet a vital personal need in your life or in the life of someone you love, but you're also a part of ministering to José in Colombia, Humberto in Chile, Gousa in India, or Lidiane in Brazil. You help make it possible for a pastor in China, a child in Peru, or a mother in West Africa to enjoy a life-changing book. And because you helped, children and adults around the world are learning God's Word and walking in his ways.

Thank you for your partnership in helping to disciple the world. May God bless you with the power of his Word in your life.

For more information about our international ministries, visit www.ccmi.org.